"*Loving Someone with an Eating Disorder* provides solid insights and clinical theory on the causes and symptoms of dysregulated eating and related body concerns, and personalizes them via case vignettes and reflective questions. Although written for partners of eating-disordered individuals, it would be equally useful for anyone who cares about someone struggling with food. I look forward to introducing my clients and their loved ones to this comprehensive, readable, and well-researched addition to our field."

—**Karen R. Koenig, LCSW, MEd**, eating disorders expert; popular blogger; and award-winning, international author of seven books on eating and weight

"*Loving Someone with an Eating Disorder* is a must-read for loved ones! Packed with key education, practical tools, and much-needed hope, Dana Harron's words will surely save relationships—and lives."

—**Jenni Schaefer**, author of *Life Without Ed*; *Almost Anorexic*; and *Goodbye Ed, Hello Me*

"There are few resources for the loved ones of those struggling with eating disorders, despite the suffering that it brings to partner relationships. This book fills that gap, bringing information, compassion, and understanding to the table, as well as practical ways for navigating the labyrinthian path towards recovery. It is a gift for those who care for someone with an eating disorder."

—**Anita Johnston, PhD**, author of *Eating in the Light of the Moon*, clinical director of Ai Pono Hawai'i, and cocreator of Light of the Moon Cafe

Loving Someone with an Eating Disorder

UNDERSTANDING, SUPPORTING & CONNECTING WITH YOUR PARTNER

DANA HARRON, PsyD

New Harbinger Publications, Inc.

Publisher's Note

This publication is designed to provide accurate and authoritative information in regard to the subject matter covered. It is sold with the understanding that the publisher is not engaged in rendering psychological, financial, legal, or other professional services. If expert assistance or counseling is needed, the services of a competent professional should be sought.

NEW HARBINGER PUBLICATIONS is a registered trademark of New Harbinger Publications, Inc.

Distributed in Canada by Raincoast Books

Copyright © 2019 by Dana Harron
      New Harbinger Publications, Inc.
      5674 Shattuck Avenue
      Oakland, CA 94609
      www.newharbinger.com

Cover design by Amy Shoup

Acquired by Jess O'Brien

Edited by Brady Kahn

Text Design by Michele Waters and Tracy Carlson

Library of Congress Cataloging-in-Publication Data on file

23   22   21

10   9   8   7   6   5   4   3   2

To my patients and their partners, who inspire me daily.

Contents

Acknowledgments

There were so many people who helped me in the preparation of this book. My husband, Ashley Harron, calmed me down, buoyed me up, and spent many sleepless nights with our newborn daughter so that I would be more prepared to write and edit. My daughter Victoria, for her part, made me feel that anything is possible. Chris and Brian, with their weekly casseroles and dishwashing, freed me up to focus on the book instead of household details. Vicraj Gill provided immense editorial support, helping me cut to the heart of the matter and to recognize which pieces are most important. I also want to acknowledge Jennifer Holder, Clancy Drake, and the ever-patient Brady Kahn for their editorial support. Jess O'Brien, my acquisitions editor, allowed me to convince him that this book is worth writing. He and Chris Teja, my erstwhile acquisitions editor, convinced me that I should be the one to write it. Melanie Gorman helped me formulate the book proposal, understand the ins and outs of the publication business, and feel supported throughout the process. Lauren Behrman helped me believe in myself and recognize the worth of my contribution. Jacqueline LaRusso and Eileen McKee both provided invaluable insights as well as editorial and emotional support. Alisa Schwartz helped me understand the impact of EDs on parenting while Tamara Pincus helped me appreciate the nuances of human sexuality. The clinicians at Monarch Wellness, as always, provided excellent patient care, which allowed me the space and time to work on this book. Finally, my patients and their partners have taught me a great deal about what they find to be helpful within their relationships, and even more about resiliency and courage.

CHAPTER 1

Loving Someone with Disordered Eating

Watching loved ones suffer, seemingly at their own hands, is one of the most painful experiences imaginable. All of the tenderness and joy of love get mixed together with rage, betrayal, and terror when an eating disorder enters the picture. It seems like you can't have all of these different feelings at once, but the most painful part is that you do. It wouldn't be so hurtful to watch your girlfriend silently leave the table to purge after a lunch date, or to watch your husband weigh himself obsessively, if you didn't also truly care about them. It would be just fine to want to shake them until they come around—punish them for the hell they've visited upon both your lives or avoid looking at them or talking to them—if your heart didn't also just break with love for them, if only once upon a time.

And there's no escaping this issue. Food is perhaps the most central aspect of every couple's daily life: we all need to eat. Additionally, food has social and emotional aspects that make it ever present in our culture. We eat to socialize, to celebrate, and to comfort. When old friends want to get together, they suggest lunch. When somebody has a birthday, we eat cake. Apology? Fruit basket. Anniversary? Dinner out. It's no wonder that it's hard for you to find your footing, for as soon as you recover from one difficult moment, the next is upon you.

The kicker is that nobody else really knows this about food. It is so much a part of everyday life that most people have the luxury of taking it completely for granted. The eating disorder (which I also refer to as ED) robs you, and your partner, of that luxury. You are now continually, painfully reminded of the role that food plays in your life every single day. Life seems so easy for everyone else who doesn't have to deal with these issues, whereas for you and your partner, everything you try feels like running into a brick wall. You also can't avoid bodies, images of bodies, ideas about how bodies "should" be, or messages about gluttony, discipline, and sloth.

If you live together, you have an additional minefield to navigate in terms of sharing a household. Grocery shopping, cooking, and eating together can take on a lot of emotional tension when an eating disorder is present. You may cook food that is never eaten or that is eaten so quickly that nothing is left for anyone else. You may be in charge of grocery shopping because of your partner's food-related anxiety. Your partner may spend exorbitant amounts of money on food, clothes, or diet plans. Treatment for eating disorders may be a financial strain, and intimacy and parenting can be affected as well.

You might feel like you don't even recognize your partner anymore. It may feel as though this is not the person you first met, or married, or had children with. An eating disorder can erode the capacity for joy, spontaneity, and emotional closeness. If you have known about your partner's eating disorder for some time, you may have hoped it would go away on its own—maybe you told yourself that it really didn't affect your relationship that much—but now the cumulative effect may have worn away at your intimacy, trust, and love. Perhaps you have suspicions but your partner denies there's a problem, or maybe your partner has acknowledged an issue but you aren't sure where to start looking for help. Or you may have only recently discovered your partner's ED, and the revelation could leave you lost and confused. Whatever the exact circumstances of your situation, this book will help you navigate the very difficult issues an eating disorder brings up, and respond with skill and compassion toward both your partner and yourself.

What follows are some indications that an eating disorder is affecting your relationship. Has anything like this happened to you?

- dreading mealtimes

- worrying about your partner's behavior a great deal of the time

- feeling responsible for your partner's food behaviors

- arguing over food situations, such as meals out, groceries, or cooking

- going out of your way to ensure that certain food items are or are not in the house

- hiding food or your own eating behaviors

- feeling used, unappreciated, or resentful when your partner struggles with food

- withdrawing and becoming unavailable

- becoming frustrated and angry as repeated attempts to "heal" or "help" fail

- making excuses for your partner's absences from social or work events

- avoiding intimacy because it triggers your partner's body shame

- feeling lonely or frustrated as your partner becomes more avoidant of intimacy

- difficulty conceiving because of the health effects of an eating disorder

- worrying that your child will not have a healthy relationship with food

If even one of these situations seems familiar, it's clear that your partner's eating disorder has an impact on your relationship—and on you. These are all very common experiences among partners of people with eating disorders. Eating disorders wreak havoc on relationships. The closer the relationship, the more trouble they cause. Don't despair, though. This book will guide you toward effective ways to deal with just these types of situations.

A Word on Gender

As you'll see in the pages that follow, eating disorders don't discriminate based upon race, ethnicity, or gender. There is ample evidence that eating disorders strike men much more often than has been previously believed; men with eating disorders are less likely to be diagnosed and treated than women are, which artificially inflates the gender disparity (Hudson et al. 2007). Because of this, I will switch back and forth between genders in this book.

You Are Not Alone

Approximately thirty million eating disorders are diagnosed in the United States every year, and many more cases go unreported (Hudson et al. 2007). People are being struck with these issues in midlife much more often than before, and this population is more likely than younger folks to be in serious and committed relationships. In other words, there are more and more partners of people with disordered eating every year. It may be helpful to review the following stories, which are composites from real partners dealing with their partner's eating disorder. While, of course, your situation is completely unique, you may see that other people's struggles are like your own in many respects. These stories include some common threads that are often present when a relationship is impacted by an eating disorder. Do they hit close to home on any level?

- *Derek's Story*

  "I knew that Jamie had bulimia in college, but I had never seen her have any issue with food since we'd been together. After we had our son, though, things changed. She began to be very negative about her body, looking at herself in the mirror with this really grossed-out look on her face all the time. Getting dressed to go somewhere started taking forever—she'd put on something, say she looked fat, and toss it in the bottom of her closet. She wasn't interested in sex at all. She said she didn't want me to see her naked until she lost weight.

  "She'd always pick the lowest calorie option when we went out to eat, but then she'd eat half of my food. It drove me crazy, but she got really defensive when I brought it up. Before very long, I noticed that she would leave for the bathroom right after meals, and that she would take a while most times. I didn't think too much of it, but then I noticed that when she came back, her eyes would be all watery and bloodshot. And sometimes she had brushed her teeth, which I thought was odd.

"We started arguing a lot of the time—it seemed like she was always in a bad mood. Sometimes it was about her body, sometimes how much money she was spending on clothes, sometimes other stuff. When she finally told me her bulimia was back, it was in the middle of a fight. I was totally stunned and surprised, but also mad. She brought it up in this way, like it was supposed to hurt me, for starters. And she had been hiding stuff from me? I kind of wondered what else she might be hiding."

• *Sara's Story*

"I thought everything was completely fine. Tim and I had been living together for a year, and we were getting along great. He is interesting, smart, and so fun to be with. At the time, he was studying for the bar exam while I worked as a nurse nearby. We were thinking about the possibility of marriage. But one day I came home a little early from doing errands, and he was in the middle of the living room with tons and tons of food and all of these empty containers all around him. Taco Bell, McDonalds, donuts, ice cream. He was completely stuffing his face, and none of this stuff had even been in the house before. He looked crazy. I froze in the doorway. I had no idea what to do or how to respond. He was clearly surprised to see me; he turned bright red and kind of stammered that it wasn't what I thought. He said he needed some time before we talked about it and went into the bedroom. I'm pretty sure I could hear him crying.

"For a long time, I've been going back and forth between pretending nothing happened and trying to ask him what the deal is. He won't talk about it. He says everything's fine and I'm making a big deal out of nothing. But I've started noticing that the grocery bills are really high sometimes and that sometimes it seems like he's trying to get me out of the house. I don't want to tell my friends or family what's going on because I'm afraid they'll think I shouldn't marry him, and I really do love him. But, to be honest, I wonder if I shouldn't get out of the relationship too sometimes. What am I signing up for here?"

• Sadie's Story

"Jackie told me about her eating disorder when we first started dating. She was in recovery, she said, but it was tenuous. She still struggled a lot with worrying about her weight, feeling very guilty and anxious if she ate something she felt she shouldn't, and letting negative thoughts about her body ruin her day. But she was such a kind and intelligent person, I hadn't met anyone like her—*If an eating disorder is part of this package*, I thought, *then so be it*. I'm certainly not perfect. I also kind of thought that I could help her to see how beautiful she is—on some level, I maybe thought I could heal her from her eating disorder.

"But nothing I say ever gets through. And, as time has gone on, I've gotten more and more worried about her. She gets anxious and upset so easily. It is so sad to watch her when she's in one of her meltdowns. I just want her to understand how wonderful she is and to stop hurting herself all the time. And, she's gotten really thin again. I think it might be time for her to go back to full-time treatment, but she says she can't take time away from work—that she can do it with just my help. So I try, but there must be some piece that I'm missing."

Taking It In

As you read these stories and reflect upon your own experience, you may be coming to realize that your partner's eating disorder actually has a tremendous impact on you, and you may feel overwhelmed. Don't worry. This book will help you make some behavioral changes that can improve how you and your partner relate as well as how you deal with the eating disorder. This book will give you a better understanding of what your partner is going through, new and healthier ways to approach your partner, and a sizable toolkit for taking good care of yourself.

Seeking Support for Yourself

It is so common for partners of people with eating disorders to feel alone. Ideally a romantic partner is our go-to person, our teammate in life. But the eating disorder puts your partner on the bench in many ways. A prime characteristic of the eating disorder is that it takes over a person's mental space; people become so preoccupied with food that it is often hard to have room for thoughts and feelings about anything else. The dictates of the eating disorder may take up an inordinate amount of time—working out, shopping for clothes, or even lying in bed because the day has gone badly. Many people find that eating disorders affect their mood negatively, as well. Even in recovery, people often need to put lots of time and energy into getting better. Eating disorders often make it hard for people to be close with others, even the ones they love.

This makes it critical that you get your own support. Reading this book is a great first step—I'll talk with you about the difficult feelings your partner's eating disorder brings up, how to relate to your partner more healthfully, and how to support your partner and yourself as you both move toward healthier ways of being. But there is no replacement for connecting with other people who understand.

Talking with others about your loved one's eating disorder can be a dicey situation with your partner sometimes; many people feel a great deal of shame about their eating disorder and hate to think of anybody else knowing about it. It's true that it's important to be respectful and to choose your sources of support carefully, but it's also true that *you will not be able to support your partner if you are not supported yourself.* It is absolutely vital that you seek out the support of friends and family, other partners, or your own therapist. Having a network of support will be good for you, and ultimately that will be good for your partner as well.

Gaining Clarity

The exercises in this book are meant to help you gain clarity about what's going on with you and with your partner and to help connect the dots between some of the abstract concepts being discussed and your actual day-to-day experiences. I'll be offering a lot of writing prompts like the following one, so it's a good idea to start keeping a journal with you as you read.

The goal of this first exercise is to give you a more complete picture of your relationship as it stands today. An eating disorder demands so much time and attention, it can be easy to lose track of how you are feeling about the relationship as a whole. Are the demands of the eating disorder too much for you to deal with, given everything else about the relationship? Would it be better to leave? Many partners find themselves asking this difficult question at one time or another.

EXERCISE 1: Thinking About Your Relationship

Use this exercise to see your partner and your relationship more clearly and to reconnect with feelings that might have gotten obscured by the presence of the eating disorder. Respond to these questions in your journal.

- *What are my nonnegotiable requirements for a relationship— the things that absolutely must be a part of any relationship that I am in? (Some examples might be safety, respect, physical attraction, or intellectual stimulation.)*

- *Are my nonnegotiable requirements met? If not, can this be changed and what would that require?*

- *What things are going well in our relationship?*

- *What are the biggest challenges we face?*

- *What personality characteristics and attributes do I love most about my partner?*

- *What personality characteristics and attributes are most difficult about my partner?*

- *What do I need to change about myself in order to be a better partner?*

- *What areas of our relationship are most affected by the eating disorder?*

- *What do I imagine our relationship would be like without the eating disorder?*

- *What issues would still be there if the eating disorder went away?*

- *What do I want our relationship to look like in the future?*

- *What has to change in order to make that possible?*

As you become clearer on the bigger picture of your relationship, you are likely to have some realizations about how to move forward. You might find that your nonnegotiable requirements are not being met now, but that they likely would be met if your partner were to be successful in recovery. If this is the case, the next question you're faced with is about how likely it is that your partner will enter a sustainable recovery. Is she currently motivated toward this end? Does she have support in place, and is she willing to seek help from professionals? If not, it might be time to have a conversation with your partner about what changes need to happen for this relationship to be successful. Please see chapter 6, which talks about effective communication, before moving forward. If you have discovered that your nonnegotiable requirements are not being met and are not likely to be met, you may be considering ending the relationship. In this case, chapter 6 will still be a good resource as you plan this difficult conversation.

If you have decided that, on the balance, this relationship is worth fighting for, then congratulations on your renewed commitment. Take a moment to write down some of the reasons why you are making this commitment so that you can refer to this list when you need a bolster later on.

Getting Educated

This chapter may have opened your eyes to just how difficult it can be to be the partner of someone who is struggling with an eating disorder. Rest assured that you're already taking the most important step right now by educating yourself. Learning about eating disorders will help you feel more grounded and less lost as you address your partner. You will learn what you are—and aren't—responsible for. You'll discover that you cannot heal your partner; you can only offer support as she tries to heal herself. You'll gain tools that can help you and your partner take care of yourselves and relate more successfully. With these goals in mind, let's press on to an overview of disordered eating in the next chapter.

CHAPTER 2

Eating Disorder Myths and Realities

So what exactly are we dealing with here? There are a lot of myths out there about eating disorders, and it's important to separate these myths from the realities. A good place to start is with the diagnostic criteria for eating disorders. Understanding your partner's diagnosis (or suspected diagnosis, if he hasn't sought treatment yet) can give you some grounding and a better idea of what's going on and what to expect. At the same time, it's important to remember that everyone is different and that everyone's eating disorder will look a little different too. The medical diagnostic system is far from perfect; many diagnoses that exist today were not recognized for years, and some diagnoses used to exist that we now realize are not mental health conditions at all.

Note that your partner likely needs and deserves help even if he does not clearly meet the full diagnostic criteria for a given eating disorder. People also often shift over time from one eating disorder diagnosis to another or have symptoms from more than one ED simultaneously. A diagnosis is best made by a professional, but if you have concerns about your partner's food behavior based upon what you read here, it is important to bring them up. Regardless of what specific diagnosis might fit your partner's behaviors, or even if none of these seems right, there is always this measuring stick: if there is some set of behaviors, attitudes, or emotional reactions that is having a substantially negative impact on your partner's life or on your relationship, then something needs to change and professional support might be helpful.

Eating Disorder Diagnoses

This section discusses the different eating disorders and the behaviors associated with each in terms of the diagnostic criteria used by professionals (American Psychiatric Association 2013). If you begin to feel overwhelmed as you're reading, be sure to take breaks and seek out other people for support. It's okay to put down the book for a little while as you process new information.

Binge-Eating Disorder

Binge-eating disorder (BED) has been around for a long time but has only recently been recognized by the psychiatric community. As you can imagine from the title, it is primarily characterized by recurrent episodes of bingeing, or eating large amounts of food in relatively short periods of time. A person may plan to binge and hit the grocery store specifically for that purpose or may feel suddenly overtaken and go through much of the food in the house. During a binge, people often feel trancelike and out of control. These episodes must meet at least three of the following criteria for a diagnosis:

- eating much more rapidly than normal

- eating until feeling uncomfortably full

- eating large amounts of food when not feeling physically hungry

- eating alone because of being embarrassed by how much you are eating

- feeling disgusted with yourself, depressed, or very guilty after overeating

The person with BED does not try to get rid of the calories in any way—this behavior would be associated with bulimia (more on this later). The bingeing must also cause distress; someone who binges and is fine with it wouldn't qualify for this diagnosis. The binges must also happen about once a week for at least three months. Of course, a great many people who don't meet this threshold are nevertheless suffering profoundly. If your loved one binges but not often enough to be diagnosed with binge-eating disorder, see the criteria for OSFED (other specified feeding and eating disorder) later in this chapter.

Binge-eating disorder is the most common eating disorder in the United States, affecting 3.5 percent of women and 2 percent of men. For women, it is more common in early adulthood as the pressures of career and family mount. Men are more likely to suffer BED during midlife. BED is extremely undertreated, with more cases than bulimia and anorexia combined but with less than 3 percent of sufferers getting treatment. Approximately one-third of people with BED have a weight within the "healthy" range (Schaffer and Robinson 2015).

Look over this list of other behaviors that are frequently associated with bingeing, keeping in mind that BED is a secretive condition; some of these things may be happening even if you haven't noticed them.

Behaviors Associated with Bingeing

- hoarding food

- hiding food

- stealing food

- running up large grocery bills

- spending money secretively

- hiding empty food containers

- lying about food

- eating in secret

- expressing shame, disgust, or self-loathing related to food

Bulimia Nervosa

Bulimia is characterized by two main behaviors: bingeing and purging. Purging is an attempt to rid the body of calories. Many people associate vomiting with bulimia, and in fact this is one of the more common forms that purging can take. Those who purge through vomiting often do it immediately after a binge, but sometimes a significant amount of time can lapse between bingeing and purging. Purging can also take other forms—some people may exercise excessively, fast for a period of time, or take diuretics or laxatives. For some people, purging feels like a necessary evil to relieve guilt about bingeing. Others find that the sense of relief and emptiness that they gain from purging is a motivation in and of itself.

Another part of the diagnosis is that a person's "self-evaluation is unduly influenced by body shape and weight" (American Psychiatric Association 2013, 345). For someone with an eating disorder, weight gain is associated with a terrible spiral of guilt, shame, and unworthiness. It can be difficult to understand why people would be so preoccupied with their body shape and size. This will be covered more in chapter 4, but for now it's enough to know that your partner's weight likely symbolizes much more to her than you can imagine. People must also be able to maintain a minimum healthy weight to qualify for the bulimia diagnosis (although they may not see their weight as healthy). One-point-five percent of American women will suffer from bulimia at some point in their lifetimes (Hudson et al. 2007).

Behaviors Associated with Purging

- anger, irritability, and/or anxiety if unable to purge after bingeing

- excusing oneself immediately after eating

- running the shower or faucet while in the bathroom

- spending an unusual amount of time in the bathroom

- returning with watery, red eyes after suspected purging

- a puffy neck or face due to swollen lymph nodes and salivary glands

- spending hours at the gym

- exercising even when injured

- fasting or dieting to compensate for food eaten

- hiding boxes of laxatives, diuretics, or enemas

- obsessing over weight, body shape, or size

Anorexia Nervosa

The typical physical features of anorexia nervosa are extreme thinness, rapid weight loss, or both. Anorexia can be quite similar to bulimia in terms of the emotional landscape, but people with anorexia are not at a healthy weight; they are too thin. Someone with anorexia may eat little (a behavior known as restriction), eat bizarrely, or exercise too much. People with anorexia are profoundly afraid of gaining weight and often obsess about this possibility; sometimes it can be difficult to think about anything else. On top of this, another feature of anorexia (and many eating disorders) is *body-image distortion*, or difficulty seeing your own body realistically. Your partner may be quite thin, even emaciated, but have difficulty fully appreciating this and even worry that she might be overweight, especially in certain body areas. (If your partner is of a healthy weight but has many of these same symptoms, see the later section that defines other specified feeding and eating disorder).

RESTRICTING TYPE AND BINGEING-PURGING TYPE

Many people think that people with anorexia never eat large volumes of food, but this is not the case. If a person only restricts and doesn't have other disordered eating behaviors, this is known as the *restricting type*. There is also a subtype of anorexia that includes bingeing and purging. Not surprisingly, this subtype is known as the *bingeing-purging type*. At some point, the starving brain overrides the fear of gaining weight, leading to a binge. Often this is followed by intense guilt and purging behaviors. The key difference between this type of anorexia and bulimia is a person's weight. If too thin, people are considered to have anorexia bingeing-purging type, but if they can maintain a healthy weight or are overweight, they are more likely to be diagnosed with bulimia.

Behaviors Associated with Restriction

- eating very little

- avoiding specific foods or food groups

- skipping meals

- obsessive calorie counting

- obsessing over fat, sugar, or other aspects of food

- cutting food into very small pieces

- eating bizarre or unusual foods or food combinations

- lying about having eaten

- obsessive weighing

- hiding food

Avoidant Restrictive Food Intake Disorder (ARFID)

Avoidant restrictive food intake disorder (ARFID) is a new diagnosis (American Psychiatric Association 2013) largely based upon the previous diagnosis known as *selective eating disorder*. It is quite similar to anorexia nervosa in terms of behaviors (reduced caloric intake, food avoidance), but the motivations are quite different. In the case of ARFID, there is no body-image disturbance or worry over body shape and size. Rather, it's the food itself that is problematic. People with ARFID may be concerned about food allergies, choking, or nausea, or may be strongly put off by the textures and tastes of many foods.

Other Specified Feeding and Eating Disorder (OSFED) and Unspecified Feeding or Eating Disorder (UFED)

If your partner doesn't neatly fit into any of the previous categories but does suffer from disordered eating behaviors, she could receive a diagnosis of other specified feeding and eating disorder (OSFED) or unspecified feeding or eating disorder (UFED). OSFED typically applies when there is an observable pattern to the eating behavior, whereas UFED is more of a catchall diagnosis for eating problems that don't fall into any other category. People who binge or who binge and purge (but not often enough to qualify for a diagnosis of binge-eating disorder or bulimia) or who restrict their food intake but for other reasons are not at a low weight (atypical anorexia) would likely receive a diagnosis of OSFED. Purging disorder, in which a person purges but doesn't binge, falls into this category, as does night eating syndrome, a condition in which people consume a large portion during the night due to a disrupted biological clock.

The following list includes the more commonly seen conditions that fall under the umbrella term of UFED but nevertheless have identifiable patterns; many of these conditions require more research to be fully understood and may eventually qualify as "other specified" or fully separate diagnoses.

ORTHOREXIA

Orthorexia is similar to anorexia in many ways, but the focus here is on the perceived healthiness of the food as opposed to its calorie content. The fear is not of gaining weight so much as of food being contaminated in some way. People with orthorexia may be overly preoccupied with avoiding pesticides or preservatives, or they may obsess over getting enough of some nutrient. This is not so-called clean eating: food preferences often become so rigid that the sufferer is not able to enjoy everyday social interactions like going out to a restaurant with friends. Ironically, orthorexia often has negative health effects for the sufferer; a very rigid diet often does not provide enough nutrient variety and balance.

MUSCLE DYSPHORIA (BIGOREXIA)

As the name implies, people with muscle dysphoria are preoccupied with the shape and size of their muscles. They may spend hours at the gym, obsess over exercise routines, and continue to push their bodies even when injured or sick. They might miss important events so they can work out, or panic if they must skip a day at the gym. Disordered patterns of eating are often a part of this picture, as diet can be seen as a part of muscle building. Some people may abuse supplements, protein, or anabolic steroids. A sufferer's sense of self-worth and lovability is overly influenced by how muscular he deems himself to be. This condition tends to affect men more than women, but women are certainly not immune.

ANOREXIA ATHLETICA (COMPULSIVE OVEREXERCISING)

In this condition, exercise becomes a primary obsession. There may be some overlap between this condition and muscle dysphoria, but in anorexia athletica the exercise is geared not toward muscle building but toward athletic performance. People with this condition may train obsessively even when injured or sick. They may be preoccupied with exercise routines and panic if they view their performance negatively. Exercise and training may interfere with social relationships, job performance, or other aspects of a well-balanced life.

COMPULSIVE OVEREATING

Compulsive overeating is often confused with binge eating, but it is different. In binge-eating disorder, people have lots of food in a discrete period of time. In compulsive overeating, people overeat generally but do not restrict their eating to particular time periods. They don't binge, per se, but they do use food for emotional reasons. Those suffering from compulsive eating are often overweight, and they may feel some shame about this. They may have undergone several failed diets, but without the emotional component of their food-use being addressed, have often returned to overeating. Another term for compulsive overeating is *emotional eating*.

Body Dysmorphic Disorder (BDD)

While not technically an eating disorder, body dysmorphic disorder warrants discussion here because it is very closely related to eating disorders. In this condition people become extremely preoccupied with real or imagined body flaws that may include height, weight, facial features, or body parts such as hips, thighs, or stomach. Sufferers from BDD are extremely self-conscious as a result, and they often frequently check their physical appearance. However, they do not engage in bingeing, purging, or restriction. If your partner suffers from BDD, especially if it is around body shape and size, many parts of this book will be relevant, because many of the emotional underpinnings of body dysmorphic disorder overlap with those of eating disorders.

The Limits of Diagnosis

Because disordered eating doesn't always fit neatly into a specific category—and people often have more than one diagnosis during their lifetime—it's often better to think in terms of disordered eating behaviors, thoughts, and feelings than to focus on a diagnosis. Mental health diagnoses exist to help professionals in the field do research and communicate with each other. They do not capture each person's unique struggle. Ultimately, any diagnosis boils down to one question: does this behavior, attitude, or emotion have a substantially negative impact on your partner's life, and does it substantially affect those around him? If the answer is yes, then you've identified a problem worth addressing regardless of the official label.

What Causes Eating Disorders?

Eating disorders are not usually caused by one single thing but rather are the result of a host of factors operating together. First, someone who eventually develops an eating disorder is often born with a genetic tendency toward it; you are more likely to develop an eating disorder if someone in your family has one.

However, environment also matters. It's like being born with a genetic tendency toward any condition or disease. If you were born with a genetic tendency toward skin cancer, you would be more likely to get it than you would be without those genes, but by wearing sunscreen and staying in the shade, you could still avoid cancer. Unfortunately, it is difficult to find shade from distorted messages about weight and food in our culture. Images of so-called perfect bodies are everywhere: on TV, in movies, in magazines, and on social media. Just walking down the street, billboards and signs constantly clamor for our attention, often depicting fit and skinny models looking happy and contented. Even if we don't pay explicit attention to these messages, they work their way into the subconscious and change what people think of as a normal body. Add to this other related cultural problems like perfectionism and rigidity, and you have an eating disorder incubator.

Sometimes, eating disorders are related to the family environment. Some families have trouble tolerating imperfections and vulnerabilities, some are overly concerned with outward appearance, and some use food as the primary method to soothe emotions. These attitudes, among others, can lead children to develop ideas about self-worth and the price of belonging that may later be expressed as an eating disorder. Be careful about pinning the blame here, though—parents often carry these beliefs because they were raised similarly.

Finally, of course, eating disorders are also caused by a person's own thought patterns, emotional landscape, and personal history. Often people who develop eating disorders have difficulty viewing themselves positively. Some may struggle with anxiety or depression and use the eating disorder as a way to manage extremely negative feelings. Some might have experienced a negative event, or trauma, which they are trying to cope with.

Chapter 4 discusses the emotional underpinnings of disordered eating in greater detail. For now, it is enough to know that eating disorders are complex and multifaceted and that every person's story is a little bit different.

Common Myths About Eating Disorders

Many people know a little bit about eating disorders, but usually a lot of what people think they know turns out to be flat wrong. Why? There are a ton of misconceptions out there, driven by movies and TV programs where the producers may be aware of the epidemic but do not devote the research dollars needed to portray eating disorders meaningfully. It's easier to describe people with eating disorders as vain, attention seeking, or willful than to delve into the complex emotional world that drives these behaviors. These myths work their way into the general population, and it wouldn't be surprising if you believe them too, even if only on some deep level. This next exercise will help you see what false beliefs you may have fallen prey to.

EXERCISE 2: Eating Disorder Myths

Read each statement, and write down whether you think it's true or false. Record your answers in your journal.

1. Only women get eating disorders.

2. Only teenagers get eating disorders.

3. Only white people get eating disorders.

4. Anybody can get an eating disorder.

5. It should be easy for people to change their eating.

6. Eating disorders have to do with emotions.

7. Eating disorders are only about food.

8. Eating disorders are not dangerous.

9. Anorexia is dangerous, but other eating disorders are not.

10. Eating disorders do not require professional treatment.

11. People do not recover from eating disorders.

12. Recovering from an eating disorder is easy.

13. Only the person diagnosed with the eating disorder needs support.

What's true or not may seem obvious at first, but on deeper examination, you may find that you are less sure about what you know or believe.

Read on to learn more about the myths and the realities.

Myth 1: Only Women Get Eating Disorders

Reality: The National Eating Disorders Association (2018a) estimates that 10 million of those receiving treatment for an eating disorder are male. The number of men who are actually suffering from disordered eating is much higher, from 25 to 40 percent of the general population according to some estimates (Hudson et al. 2007).

Men are much less likely than women to seek treatment for eating disorders. There's a huge stigma surrounding the idea of having a "girl's disease," so getting help can be riddled with shame. Also, disordered eating may look very different for males, who have different "ideal" body types manufactured and promoted to them by diet and fitness industries. Muscle dysmorphia is most common among men and is one of the least discussed eating disorders around.

Myth 2: Only Teenagers Get Eating Disorders

Reality: Eating disorders in midlife are increasingly common and growing at an alarming rate. According to a 2013 study by Diann Ackard and others, eating disorder rates in midlife rose 11.6 percent between 2002 and 2006. When this trend is compared to the 4.7 percent increase between 1989 and 2001, it becomes clear that eating disorders in midlife are rising exponentially. Thirteen percent of women over fifty have disordered eating symptoms (Gagne et al. 2012). There is less information available on men in midlife for the reasons already stated, but I would bet that eating disorders are much, much more common in middle-aged men than people think.

Midlife has unique stressors, such as raising children and supporting aging parents, work stress, and household responsibilities. In the current cultural climate, ideas like "fifty is the new thirty" increase the pressure to maintain a certain body type during this stressful time, even as the body slows its metabolism, changes its chemistry, and responds differently to food and exercise. For many women, having children can change the body significantly as well. For men, lowered testosterone contributes to similar changes. Add to this all of the cultural messages about what it means to become "old," and you have a recipe for disaster.

Myth 3: Only White People Get Eating Disorders

Reality: It is true that different races and ethnicities may have different body ideals, and that a curvier body may be more acceptable in some cultures than others. However, many people think that this makes certain groups somehow immune to eating disorders, and this is not at all the case. Eating disorders are not only about body shape and size. They often evolve as ways of managing high levels of stress, often including negative thoughts and feelings about self. In our dominant culture, which pushes not only a *thin ideal* (the idea that thin is better than not thin) but also a *white ideal*, these thoughts and feelings might even be much worse among some people of color, who experience daily racism and discrimination. A 2013 review of studies focusing on this topic showed both that ethnic minorities were less likely to seek treatment for disordered eating and that referrers were significantly less likely to send ethnic minorities to specialists in disordered eating (Sinha and Warfa 2013).

Myth 4: It Should Be Easy for Your Partner to Change

Reality: Because eating disorders are observed in terms of a person's behavior with food, you may think that it would be easy to stop the behavior and therefore stop the disorder. But the motivations behind eating-disordered behaviors are immensely powerful and often overwhelm a person's reason. Rational arguments don't always work with emotionally-based or ingrained patterns. It would be like if you suffered from insomnia, and somebody said to you, "Well, just go to sleep!" Eating disorders are caused by a complex interaction of genetic, environmental, and social factors, and they require treatment at many levels.

Myth 5: Eating Disorders Are Only About Food

Reality: An eating disorder is about using food and the body as a way to cope with deep and complex emotional issues. The exact psychological reasons behind disordered eating behavior are different for everyone. It may be about numbing anger or coping with shame. Sometimes it's a way to try to feel good enough when that feeling is hard to find. The rules of the eating disorder often feel to the sufferer like they were written in stone—it really doesn't seem to be okay to eat after a certain time of night, to have seconds, or to stop exercising before the clock has reached whatever-o'clock. Following these food rules is done for deep psychological reasons. For more on this, see chapter 4.

Myth 6: Eating Disorders Are Not Dangerous

Reality: The unfortunate reality is that eating disorders can be quite dangerous. The behaviors associated with these diseases are very hard on the body and can have extremely serious consequences. Restriction, or not eating enough to fuel the body's needs, can lead to slow heart rate, low blood pressure, and even heart failure. Osteoporosis, or brittle bones, is often caused by not having enough calcium. Dehydration is quite common with restriction and may lead to kidney issues. Malnutrition can also cause further mental health problems or make existing ones worse.

Purging can have severe health consequences as well, including electrolyte imbalances that can lead to heart failure. If a person is purging by vomiting, the esophagus can become inflamed and may even rupture. If someone is using laxatives, the gastrointestinal tract can stop functioning properly and the person can become severely dehydrated (again, possible kidney failure). Peptic ulcers and pancreatitis are associated with purging as well. The health consequences of bingeing are largely those associated with clinical obesity, such as high cholesterol, high blood pressure, and type 2 diabetes. In addition, the uncontrolled nature of the binge may lead to a gastric rupture, a tear in the stomach that can potentially be fatal.

Myth 7: Eating Disorders Do Not Require Professional Treatment

Reality: Because eating disorders are so complex—involving emotions, behaviors, and physical consequences—attempting to deal with an ED on your own can be difficult and potentially harmful. It is absolutely vital to work with a team who knows the terrain, often a psychotherapist, dietitian, medical doctor, and perhaps a psychiatrist. Attempting recovery on your own after a prolonged period of restriction can even be dangerous, because the body may have difficulty adjusting to having normal amounts of food again. Having food intake monitored by a professional is important to make sure that recovery doesn't put the body through more trauma.

Additionally, as previously discussed, the emotional factors involved in eating disorders are multifaceted and deep. A spouse, boyfriend, or girlfriend can never be the only support for someone working through these types of issues—you are just too close to the problem. Psychotherapists who specialize in eating disorders are trained to know what to look for and what questions to ask. They also bring value as an objective outside party without the same type of stake in the outcome. Without treatment, up to 20 percent of people with serious eating disorders die. With treatment, that number falls to 2 to 3 percent (Anorexia Nervosa and Related Disorders 2018). If your partner has not yet sought treatment, pay special attention to chapter 6, which discusses how to encourage your partner to get help.

Myth 8: People Do Not Recover from Eating Disorders

Reality: Although people who have had eating disorders would be wise to avoid potential triggers like diets for the rest of their lives (as would the rest of us!), about 60 percent of people with eating disorders recover with proper treatment (Anorexia Nervosa and Related Eating Disorders 2018). Recovery is a hard process, and it does not move forward in a straight line; there are backward steps and pitfalls all along the way. But, with help, many sufferers do eventually break free of the prison of the eating disorder and reestablish healthy relationships with their bodies, their selves, and the loved ones in their lives.

Myth 9: You Don't Need Help

Reality: Dealing with your partner's eating disorder is a tremendous strain, and you probably need more support than you presently have. Your partner may be unavailable to you in a variety of ways, and even when you can lean on your partner, you cannot be as frank and candid about the ED's impact on you as you would be with an objective outsider. It is virtually impossible to support other people well when you do not have the support that you need.

EXERCISE 3: Eating Disorder Myths Review

Now that you have learned more about the myths and realities of eating disorders, take this quiz again.

True or false? Record your answers in your journal.

1. Only women get eating disorders.

2. Only teenagers get eating disorders.

3. Only white people get eating disorders.

4. Anybody can get an eating disorder.

5. It should be easy for people to change their eating.

6. Eating disorders have to do with emotions.

7. Eating disorders are only about food.

8. Eating disorders are not dangerous.

9. Anorexia is dangerous, but other eating disorders are not.

10. Eating disorders do not require professional treatment.

11. People do not recover from eating disorders.

12. Recovering from an eating disorder is easy.

13. Only the person diagnosed with the eating disorder needs support.

Conclusion

Now you have learned a great deal about eating disorders, the behaviors that go along with them, and the ways they can impact your relationship. The chapters that follow will delve into what to do about these difficult issues. You may be surprised to learn that the best way to start helping your partner is to take good care of yourself! Let's forge ahead.

CHAPTER 3

How Your Partner's Eating Disorder Affects You

Now that you have a little bit more information about what your partner may be going through, let's talk about you again. Why? It's like that warning about what to do in case of an emergency landing: put on your own oxygen mask before you try to help anyone else. Unless you are conscious and awake yourself—making sure that you're meeting all of your own needs—you can't help others. So you need to make sure that you are in a mentally healthy place before you can support your partner effectively. As you'll see, the eating disorder is likely to have taken a toll on you too.

A Plethora of Feelings

Any situation as complex as loving somebody with an eating disorder is bound to stir up lots of feelings, even emotions that do not seem as though they should be able to coexist. Having a handle on how you are feeling will help you know what you need and what you need to do. If you are aware of sadness, for example, this might tip you off that you need more support and connection. If you become aware of anger, this might mean that you need better boundaries. Unacknowledged feelings don't just go away, either. They hang out in the background, doing damage to both you and your relationship as they come out in all kinds of insidious ways. Passive aggression, taking out your anger on the wrong people, or setting yourself up to be a doormat all come from not being clear about how you feel.

EXERCISE 4: Identifying Your Feelings

In your journal, describe how you feel when it comes to your partner's struggle. You can choose words from the list that follows, or come up with your own. You don't have to write a whole paragraph or even write in complete sentences. Simply identifying the feelings is helpful.

angry	disgusted	betrayed
helpless	afraid	protective
in shock	enraged	tender
loving	sad	lost
worried	embarrassed	longing
uncertain	suspicious	frustrated
hopeless	ashamed	jealous
lonely	contemptuous	confused
guilty	exhausted	isolated
apathetic	irritated	hurt
hostile	critical	selfish
anxious	panicked	dreading
grieving	concerned	relieved
bewildered	inadequate	exasperated
responsible	disappointed	hopeless
scared	loved	nervous
sympathetic	dejected	discouraged
despairing	optimistic	confident
indifferent	drained	hated

pressured	worthless	stressed
paralyzed	encouraged	motivated
forgotten	lost	alone
numb	empty	contemptuous

You likely have more feelings, and more complex feelings, than you might have recognized before. Getting clear about them will keep them from getting in your way.

Now that you have identified many of your feelings, you may see that your emotional experience is extremely complex. This is completely normal. Many people think that they aren't supposed to feel different or contradictory emotions at the same time, but we all do, especially if we are dealing with a partner who has an eating disorder. The next thing that you will hopefully take away from this exercise is a sense of self-compassion. If you had a friend you really cared about who told you that she was having all of the feelings you identified, what would you say? Wouldn't you think that it sounded like a lot to deal with and also that your friend probably needed some extra care right now? This leads to the third takeaway from this exercise: what you are dealing with is extremely difficult and complex, so taking care of yourself is the most important thing to do right now.

Let's explore some common feelings in more detail so that you can get a better sense of the expected emotional terrain.

Love

Love is the most important feeling we have as human beings, and without it, all of the other feelings you are having would be much less complex. You might feel that your love for your partner remains untainted by the eating disorder, and if so, that can be a tremendous source of strength when things get difficult. It is also normal to sense that your love is covered up by other, conflicting emotions—even though you know it is there, it is difficult to access sometimes. Maybe some of the things that you love about your partner—her passion or his dedication—are entangled in the eating disorder. This can feel complicated, but remember that it is okay to respect, admire, and even love a trait in a person while also hating how that trait is being used. In other words, it is okay to have complicated feelings.

" I love Amanda, but sometimes I don't feel like this person *is* Amanda."—*Marius, partner*

"Jerry seems to hate it that I love him, because it doesn't fit in with the way he sees himself."—*Pat, partner*

"I love Jessie, but sometimes I wish that I didn't." —*Jennifer, partner*

Fear

Eating disorders have serious health consequences, and it's normal to have some fear about what these might be for your partner. It is okay to acknowledge your fears and to express them to your partner in a healthy and constructive way, but do not expect your partner to make real or lasting changes to his behavior as a result. You might expect that your partner will fear the same consequences you fear, but the eating disorder does mental tricks that make it difficult for your partner to grapple with the dangers of this behavior. And changes made based upon fear—your own or others'—are rarely sustainable anyway.

Your fears are likely not just about health. You might worry that the disorder will destroy your relationship, affect your partner's parenting, or cost your family more than you can afford. It is normal to be concerned about these issues and, again, it is appropriate and healthy to share your concerns with your partner. At the same time, it is important to manage your expectations about what your partner will do with this information; the thoughts and feelings the ED provokes can sometimes make it difficult to take in feedback.

"I am afraid that Judy is going to die before she gets help." —*Jacob, partner*

"I worry that we will go bankrupt with a million failed treatments."—*Ying, partner*

"I don't know what this means for our future, and I'm afraid to find out."—*Suzanne, partner*

Anger

When somebody we love is hurting we naturally feel angry, especially if the cause of the hurt seems unnecessary or avoidable. And so when your partner hurts herself through the eating disorder, of course you have an angry reaction. You might also get angry when the eating disorder makes it hard for the two of you to relate or makes it difficult to live your lives normally, or even when it's just gotten really annoying.

It's okay to be angry, and it's okay to communicate that anger. What often gives people trouble is that the anger needs to be communicated in a healthy and constructive way. Yelling, stomping, or being passive aggressive are not okay—these behaviors not only harm your relationship but keep you from feeling good about yourself. Constructive angry behaviors, such as setting boundaries or having honest discussions with your partner, benefit everyone involved.

"It's so infuriating that he has these ideas about food that are just plain wrong, and he is so stubborn about them!"—*Jessie, partner*

"I get really fed up with Dominique. Everything's got to be so difficult, we can't just relax and have fun."—*Imani, partner*

"It's like Janet doesn't even care about her health or what this is doing to me and the kids."—*Jacob, partner*

Handling Strong Feelings

Chances are good that you have identified many feelings at this point, and that at times these feelings may feel quite overwhelming to you. Here are some helpful tips for handling the staggering array of intense emotions that are a normal part of being in this difficult situation.

BE CLEAR ABOUT YOUR FEELINGS

I once worked with a man who had a terrible road-rage incident on the way to see his wife at treatment—he berated the other driver, threatened him, and even kicked his car. It was only later in therapy that he came to see that he had really been angry about his wife's eating disorder and that it was coming out in surprising ways. To figure out how you're really feeling, take some time to slow down and pay attention to what is going on in your body. Talk it over with a friend or a therapist, or write about it in your journal.

APPRECIATE THAT COMPLICATED FEELINGS ARE NORMAL

It might feel like you're going crazy sometimes. You may feel so numb that you don't seem to experience much of anything, or you may swing from one extreme to the other. This is all totally normal given the situation you're in. Telling yourself how you *should* feel is just about as helpful as telling yourself whether you should be tired or not. Emotions are not choices or moral concepts: they just happen.

UNDERSTAND THAT FEELINGS ARE DIFFERENT FROM BEHAVIORS

Many times people are afraid to acknowledge their feelings. They are reluctant to admit that they feel angry, for example, because they don't want to yell at people and carry on. This is where the distinction between feelings and behaviors becomes extremely important. Certainly you would not want to have an important discussion while you are feeling extremely angry; no one is in the right frame of mind to communicate clearly and lovingly when feeling that way. But feeling angry isn't the same as acting angry. When you feel angry, you can acknowledge that emotion internally and see what you can learn from it.

LET IT OUT, APPROPRIATELY

You might have heard that it doesn't do any good to bottle up emotions, and that's true. At the same time, it doesn't do any good to let your emotions spill out willy-nilly all over anyone who happens to be nearby. It can be helpful to start processing your emotions in ways that you know won't be damaging to your relationship: writing in a journal, talking to a friend, or just taking long walks to think about what's going on with you. When you spend this type of time with your feelings, often you can come up with constructive ways to use the information that they are giving you. To keep with the previous example of being angry, after you've cooled down, you can use the information that the anger gave you to have a constructive conversation. You can tell people what's bothering you, and you might implement better boundaries. Read chapter 6 on communication before giving this a try, though!

Matching Baggage

Just about all of us want our partners to understand us. This is why people who struggle with mental health issues often find each other. People with anxiety, depression, substance abuse, or eating issues often feel connected to others who are familiar with those problems or with the feelings associated with them. If this is the case for you, and you are aware of it, then you're ahead of the game. You already know that handling your own issues is an important part of a healthy relationship. Many people are not fully aware of their struggles, though, so the exercise below is designed to help illuminate any problem areas.

EXERCISE 5: Honest Investigations

Please take the screening tools for each of the three areas listed in this exercise, even if you think that there isn't anything going on with you in that area. If you agree with any of these statements, write them down in your journal.

Food and Body Concerns

I skip meals in order to lose weight.

I tell others I have eaten when I haven't.

I eat in secret.

I feel like how you eat makes you a good or bad person.

I ignore being hungry.

I frequently go on diets.

I weigh myself quite often.

I think about my weight, shape, or size much of the time.

I have lost or gained a significant amount of weight without a medical problem.

I intentionally vomit to manage weight.

I feel guilty or ashamed when I eat.

I take diuretics or laxatives to control my weight.

I often eat because I am sad, angry, or lonely, even if I'm not hungry.

I have trouble stopping eating even when I feel full.

I feel out of control around food.

The way I see my body is very different from the way that other people see it.

I feel guilty or panicked if I cannot exercise.

I exercise even when I am injured or ill.

Now add up the number of statements that are true for you. If the number is zero, you likely have a healthy relationship with food, exercise, and your body. If even one of these statements is true for you, it would be good to talk with a professional, because food-and-body concerns may be a problem area for you.

Again, read the following statements for signs of depression, recording any statement that is true for you.

Depression

I feel hopeless most of the time.

I have begun sleeping a great deal more than before.

I have begun sleeping much less than usual.

My appetite has changed recently.

I feel down and blue.

I don't enjoy things that I used to enjoy.

I have no energy.

I don't spend time socializing like I used to.

I don't like myself.

I feel worthless.

I think about suicide or death.

I cry much of the time.

I feel agitated and irritable.

Add up the total number of statements that are true for you. If even one of these is true, it is possible that you are struggling with some depressive feelings, and it would be a good idea to check in with a professional. The more statements you have endorsed, the more important it will be to check in with someone.

Finally, read the following statements associated with anxiety and record any statement that is true for you.

Anxiety

I have trouble sleeping.

My thoughts seem to race, jumping from one worry to another.

Sometimes my heart beats so fast that I think I'm having a heart attack.

My muscles are often clenched.

I worry a lot.

I have frequent stomachaches.

Sometimes I feel panicked and out of control.

I feel that everything has to be perfect.

I am unable to relax.

Sometimes I cannot let a thought or worry go.

I worry about getting everything done.

Add up the total number of statements that are true for you. If you've rated any statement as true, it might be helpful to check in with a professional. The more statements you have rated as true, the more important it will be for you to seek help.

If you've uncovered any issues of your own through these exercises, you will need to address them before trying to support your partner. Each of these issues prevents people from being able to be a good source of support for others. I suggest the assistance of a professional and, if you have identified food issues, then choose a professional who is specifically trained in this area.

Taking Care of Yourself

At this point you have a sense of what you are dealing with. Maybe you've identified a problem such as anxiety or depression that you would benefit from treating. Hopefully you've been able to acknowledge the difficult and complex feelings that having a partner with an eating disorder can cause. Realizing this will help you in a number of ways. It will make it clear that your partner is not the only one with a problem: just the fact that your partner has an ED means you are dealing with something that is clearly a significant stressor. This understanding might help you find more empathy for your partner and reconceptualize the eating disorder as something that you and your partner are trying to attack together. In this way, it can ultimately bring you closer together. Perhaps more importantly, seeing how difficult your position is will hopefully make it clear that you must take extremely good care of yourself.

Why Self-Care Comes First

You are in a terribly difficult situation that even somebody operating at maximum capacity would have trouble navigating. If you are also tired, stressed, or overwhelmed, this will inevitably affect your ability to be a good support to your partner. You can't pour from an empty cup.

For the purposes of illustration, think about a time when you were your worst self—nasty, argumentative, or rude. Why did you act that way? Were you taking good care of yourself at the time? I bet you probably weren't. Now remember a time that you were your best self—generous, forgiving, and genuinely caring. How were you feeling at the time? Usually people say that they are able to treat others well when they themselves are feeling well. When you are taking good care of yourself, you're also making yourself available to take good care of your partner. When you are tired, stressed out, or sick—guess what? You won't act like your best self, and you are not likely to be a good support to your partner.

Self-Care Basics

Self-care is more of an attitude than any particular set of behaviors. Engaging in self-care is first about deciding that the way you treat yourself is a priority in your life. Some components of self-care can include caring for your body, caring for your relationships, and caring for your home. And sometimes self-care means letting some of these things go when you need to rest and relax.

EXERCISE 6: Self-Care Assessment

A good place to start is to examine how well you are taking care of yourself already in these fundamental areas: physical care, relational care, emotional care, and domestic care. Using your journal, rate yourself on a scale of 1 to 5, where 1 means rarely and 5 means all the time, as to how true each of the statements is for you in these areas.

1. **Physical Care: I...**

    Keep my body clean

    Wear clean and comfortable clothes that fit

    Eat when I am hungry

    Stop eating when I am full

    Drink as much water as my body needs

    Sleep as much as my body needs

    Brush teeth and floss regularly

Get medical and dental check ups

Attend to illnesses or injury

2. **Relational Care: I...**

Have a network of friends that I can do fun things with

Have a network of friends that I can rely on emotionally

Balance spending time with others and spending time alone

Establish healthy boundaries and stick to them

Am honest with others who are important to me

Communicate clearly in relationships

Say no when I need to

Spend time with people I like

Keep in touch with people whose relationship I value

3. **Emotional Care: I...**

Take time to pay attention to how I am feeling

Treat my feelings like they are important

Regularly talk to a friend, family member, or professional about my emotions

Have healthy and constructive outlets for anger

Comfort myself when I am feeling sad

Allow myself to cry when I am sad

Generally know whether I am in a bad or a good mood

Talk to myself in a loving and compassionate manner

Spend time doing things I enjoy

Consider myself to be responsible with my own happiness

4. **Domestic Care: I...**

Keep my environment clean

Keep my environment comfortable

Don't clutter my environment with too many things

Fix things relatively quickly when they break

Pay bills shortly after they arrive

Ensure that there is adequate lighting for me to see

Maintain a comfortable temperature in the home

It's great if you are already taking good care of yourself, but don't beat yourself up if you rated yourself low in these areas of self-care. Instead try to use what you've learned to make improvements that will help you and, ultimately, your partner.

Remember, taking good care of yourself relates directly to how stable and centered you feel. This is an important goal in its own right, but feeling grounded also makes you able to be supportive of your partner.

EXERCISE 7: My Self-Care Plan

What are some specific ways to improve self-care that you can start doing right now? Write in your journal about what you plan to do in each of these domains: physical, relational, emotional, and domestic.

Because self-care is a journey, not a destination, it's important to regularly check in with yourself about how you are doing. Set an alarm in your phone, right now, that will go off in a month to remind you to revisit this page and see if you've made the headway you expected. If you have, fantastic! What are the next steps that you can take to keep improving how you feel? If you haven't come as far as you'd hoped, go easy on yourself and see what it would take to reapply yourself to this problem.

As you move forward to understand your partner's struggle more deeply, keep self-care in mind. When you are taking better care of yourself, you are more able to access empathy for what other people are experiencing.

CHAPTER 4

Finding Empathy to Support Real Healing

How does your empathy help your partner? A sense of where others are coming from informs an understanding of what they need from you. When you have a deeper understanding of what's going on with your partner, you will find yourself naturally moving toward a more healthy and supportive stance. As you find the right balance between empathy and the principles of good self-care that you learned in chapter 3, you will begin to form healthier boundaries so that you can approach your partner supportively without sacrificing your sense of well-being and allowing guilt and resentment to build.

EXERCISE 8: The Power of Perception

The first thing to keep in mind is that your partner really does come by her way of viewing food honestly. She isn't trying to be difficult or make life hard—she really and truly feels terribly about herself, her body, and her food. Sometimes the eating disorder completely takes over, and your partner believes 100 percent of what it has to say. Other times, she may seem to switch back and forth from having an awareness of what's really going on and falling into the eating disorder traps. She may even simultaneously know and not know the reality of the situation. Think of it as an optical illusion, another place that your brain might play tricks on you.

Look at the optical illusion in figure 1. Which line is longer?

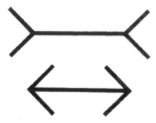

Figure 1: Optical Illusion

The objective truth is that these lines are the same length! You can take a ruler and measure them if you'd like. But knowing that they're the same length doesn't really change the way you perceive them, does it? Now, imagine somebody telling you *not* to see the lines as different lengths, that it's stupid of you to think that the lines are different lengths or that you aren't trying hard enough to see that the lines are the same length. Wouldn't that feel terrible? And, would it change the way that the image appears to you? Of course not.

This experience is a little like having an eating disorder. No matter how many people tell you that your perceptions are incorrect, and even if you know on some level that the way you're seeing things isn't entirely realistic, it's really hard to let it go. It seems true—even if you simultaneously know it isn't true—that your value is determined by your food behaviors, that your worth hinges on your body size, and that your lovability is about following food and exercise rules.

Respecting Your Partner's Experience

The previous exercise shows that arguing the facts of the case with your partner won't get you anywhere and in fact may make things worse. Using empathy, trying to understand the way that your partner sees things even though you don't agree, is a better approach.

One couple I worked with illustrates this idea perfectly. When Bria had trouble with a meal, Michael got frustrated and started trying to convince her not to be so anxious. Unfortunately, this made Bria more anxious. So, of course, she had an even more difficult time eating. It was a vicious cycle. Michael and Bria were arguing or sitting in cold angry silence at almost every meal they shared.

In therapy, Michael came to see that this dynamic was leaving Bria unsupported and was not helping matters. It made it so that Bria and Michael felt like they weren't on the same team. Eventually, Bria was able to explain to Michael that although she rationally knew that it's important to eat well, and although she wished that it were easier, it was still making her really anxious. When Michael was able to really understand where Bria was coming from, he changed from trying to convince her to trying to support her. We practiced new ways to approach Bria, such as asking what would be helpful for her and helping her slow her breathing down. Before long, Bria's anxiety decreased, and she was able to feel more like Michael was on her side.

EXERCISE 9: Seeds of Empathy

In your journal, write out responses to the prompts below. This exercise should give you more empathy for what your partner is going through and help you think about how to better approach her.

1. What was a time that you had a concern that other people didn't share or understand? It may have been an experience of anxiety, such as flying, claustrophobia, or a fear of heights, or a time when you were upset by something that other people didn't think you should be upset about.

2. How did you need and want other people to approach you about this topic?

3. Are there ways in which you can use this experience to begin to understand how your partner feels about food-and-body concerns?

Understanding Your Partner's Eating Disorder

A deeper sense of what your partner experiences on a daily basis will help you understand how to approach him. What follows are some common aspects of eating disorders that will give you insight into your partner's experience. Of course, everyone is different, so talk with your partner about whether or not these ideas fit (you may want to review chapter 6 on good communication first).

The Importance of Food

Food has an extremely different meaning for your partner than it does for you. People with eating disorders have difficulty thinking of food as only one important part of their lives; it comes to represent much more. As the eating disorder progresses, thoughts and feelings about food—eating it, not eating it, thinking about eating it, getting rid of it, avoiding it, wanting it, not wanting it, and craving it—become more and more important. Food may even become the guiding principle for how your partner is living his life. Dealing with food often becomes more important than everything else, even you. This isn't because you are actually unimportant to your partner or because your love has no meaning; it is just what the disorder does.

The essence of the disorder is to make thoughts and feelings about food grow out of control until there isn't much space left for anything else. Ask people with an eating disorder if they've had a good day, and they will mentally review what they ate. If they feel like they ate well (not too much and not the wrong things), then it's a good day. If they feel like they broke their rules about food or gave into urges to binge, it's a bad day. Other factors don't really merit. Food comes to occupy such a powerful role that, without treatment, people are willing to lose their relationships, their jobs, and even their health to satisfy the eating disorder's demands.

"It feels like I have a drill sergeant inside my head who is always yelling at me. Don't eat that! Exercise more!"
—*Lonnie, suffering from anorexia*

"All I have room to think about is food."
—*Ben, diagnosed with bulimia*

The Inescapability of Food

If you had a problem with alcohol, although it might be difficult, you could stop drinking. The same goes for many other addictions, such as gambling or narcotics. You could quit, because none of these things is essential to life. But you can't stop eating food. So people with eating disorders are confronted multiple times a day with the very thing that makes them feel the most insecure, anxious, and uncertain of themselves. Remember, too, that you always carry your body around. You are never, ever, not for a single moment, without it! There is always an opportunity to look down and evaluate what you see—and an opportunity for the eating disorder to make you feel like it isn't good enough. The inescapability of food and the body makes eating disorders a particularly difficult nemesis to combat. It's a disorder that you can't get away from.

"I am continually having some inner dialogue about whether or not I'm fat. I don't get a moment's peace."
—*Jerry, struggling with bulimia*

"Good" and "Bad" Foods

As important as how much food people with an eating disorder feel comfortable eating is what foods they feel comfortable eating. People with eating disorders often rigidly define foods as either good or bad. "Good" foods typically include vegetables, fruits, and other low calorie options. "Bad" foods (also known as *fear* foods) are high calorie foods, desserts, or other foods that don't feel safe to eat. As someone gets increasingly sick, the scope of foods that feel safe to eat becomes more and more narrow. I once worked with a woman who would have a bowlful of olives every night for dinner—any other choice made her feel too overwhelmed and anxious.

Think about what it would be like if somebody asked you to eat something that you would never, ever consider eating—that even felt unsafe or dangerous for you to have. Imagine it was dirt, or maybe even poison! The sense of anxiety and disgust that you would have is similar to what people with an eating disorder experience when you ask them to eat a food that they consider bad. You might think, *Hold on a minute. This isn't dirt, and it isn't poison—it's a piece of pie!* But remember the optical illusion exercise? The eating disorder makes the food seem to be a really dangerous thing to your partner, whether or not she wishes it did and no matter what logic has to say about it. Understanding this will help you approach your partner with more understanding and sensitivity when she is dealing with a fear food.

> "When I try to eat something with fats or sugars in it,
> there's always an idea in the back of my head like it's really
> just wrong, even though I know I need to gain weight."
> —*Jonelle, struggling with anorexia*

The Experience of ED Behaviors

Disordered eating behaviors have specific mental effects on your partner, and learning about these effects will help you understand your partner's experience.

The Effects of Restriction

The mental energy of people with eating disorders is consumed with thoughts about food eaten and calories burned. This takes on a special importance when people are not eating enough, because their mental energy is often lower than normal—the brain needs enough nutrition to function properly. People who don't have enough food can become depressed and hysterical. This was proven in the 1950s with the Minnesota Starvation Experiment, which was designed to study what we would be up against in the case of a famine. Researchers deprived thirty-six healthy men of food by severely restricting their diet for a period of twenty-four weeks and found that the effects were staggering. The men became listless, irritable, and anxious. They couldn't concentrate on anything, couldn't remember things, and couldn't really even understand what was going on around them much of the time. One participant cut off some of his fingers with an ax. Remember, these men were totally healthy and normal before the experiment. The participants also developed an extreme preoccupation with food, which may explain why many anorexic people spend hours poring over cookbooks and preparing elaborate meals for other people to eat (Keys et al. 1950).

Even while these profound effects are happening, people who are restricting sometimes report that they are not hungry. Sometimes this may be a fabrication, because eating feels too overwhelming and scary. Other times, though, it represents an honest assessment. There comes a certain point in the development of an eating disorder where the body begins to have trouble knowing when it needs food, so people may truly not get the signal that they are hungry even though their bodies are starving. This is known as *losing your hunger cues*. Luckily, hunger cues can come back with adequate nutrition during recovery.

Restricting can also make people feel irritable. They may be chronically cold no matter how high you turn up the heat or how many layers of clothing they put on. And they may put on lots of layers; many people with eating disorders feel a desire to hide their body from others. It might hurt for someone who has lost too much weight to sit down because there is not enough padding around the bones, and a woman might lose her period, as reproductive hormones are diminished by malnutrition.

> "There's always a mental tally in my head of what I ate. Pretty
> frequently, I lose track or worry that I've missed something,
> so I'm constantly adding it up in my head, over and over again."
> —*Samuel, diagnosed with OSFED*

> "I am always cold, tired, and irritable."
> —*Jennifer, struggling with anorexia*

The Effects of Bingeing

People who binge often describe a state of numbness or of being "zoned out" during the process. Restriction is a particularly common setup for bingeing because the starving brain can make you crave high calorie, high-fat foods. Many people restrict throughout the day and then end up bingeing at night because of this, a process known as a *binge-restrict cycle*. Other people will plan on bingeing and may even look forward to it throughout the day, considering the anticipation an important part of the process. Still others make plans to eat normally and then find themselves in a binge when their emotional resources break down. They may not be fully aware of what they are doing.

During a binge, people go through an extremely large amount of food. Sometimes going to get binge foods is an important part of the process, and sometimes the urge to binge overtakes people at home so that they go through all or most food available there. You can see how this would lead to poor boundaries around food that is intended for other people. It can also lead to eating bizarre food or food combinations at times; many patients I've worked with have routinely eaten jars of peanut butter or whole boxes of cereal. Sometimes people have specific foods that they always go to when they are bingeing, their "binge foods" that they crave deeply.

Bingeing makes people feel painfully full and may result in severe digestive problems. After bingeing, it may be difficult to do anything other than lie down. People often also have tremendous guilt and shame about bingeing, and it may seem to some that the terrible feeling of fullness is a deserving punishment for their behavior. Some people seek out this feeling of fullness because, although it is uncomfortable, it provides them with emotional security for psychological reasons.

> "I don't know what happens to me. I think, *Oh, it's okay if
> I have a cookie or two*, and it's like the next thing I know,
> I've torn through the whole bag and then another one to boot."
> —*Annie, diagnosed with binge-eating disorder*

> "When I'm in a binge-zone, I don't care about anything.
> I'll steal my husband's food without thinking twice about it—
> although I'll feel really bad later, at the time, it feels almost like
> life or death."—*James, diagnosed with binge-eating disorder*

The Effects of Purging

For many people, purging is a way to get rid of the calories and the guilt that result from a binge. Purging is like paying penance for the enjoyment that they had during the binge phase. Many people believe that they won't gain any weight if they purge after bingeing. (This tactic ultimately does not keep weight off, but they believe it will, because of either the wiles of the eating disorder or just plain misinformation.)

For other people, purging is a source of gratification in its own right. Some people describe purging through vomiting "cathartic release," much like finally going to the bathroom after a long period of time. Many appreciate the empty, shaky feeling that results from vomiting. Purging can also be done through fasting, exercise, diuretics, or caffeine pills; different feelings associated with each of these methods can have their own addictive qualities.

> "Purging is my super-power. Other people have to get fat if they eat like I do, but I have this special trick."
> —*Zoe, struggling with bulimia*

> "Once I'm done going through all the food in the house, I panic. I feel like I have to get rid of it, or I'm going to be so fat."
> —*Jason, struggling with bulimia*

Emotional Underpinnings of Eating Disorders

Why does food begin to take up so much mental energy for your partner? For somebody with an eating disorder, food becomes attached to powerful emotions. Perhaps the most important thing for you to learn about eating disorders is that at the same time that it is completely about food, body, and weight, it is also *not about those things at all*. Food is a way to manage chaotic, profoundly negative feelings. The body is like a stage on which some emotional drama is played out, often involving themes about deeply personal questions surrounding love, belonging, and worth.

Now, it's important to note that we are not discussing this so that you can go and play therapist with your partner! This would cause more harm than good. But a basic understanding of your partner's emotional experience can help you to meet him with a little more compassion—after all, we all understand what it's like to feel bad.

Shame

While people with eating disorders can have any size or shape body, one thing is fairly universal: a deep sense of shame about it. For some, this means hyper-focusing on a specific body part such as hips or legs. For others, the feeling is more global. People with eating disorders may literally see themselves as larger than they are, or it may be more that they have skewed perceptions about what it means to be thin, fat, round, or thick. Many people describe concerns about whether or not other people see them as fat and also a bodily sensation that has more of an inner focus, a sensation they call "feeling fat."

Body shame is usually connected to a deeper sense of shame about the self as a whole. Shame researcher Brené Brown (2014) describes shame as "as the intensely painful feeling or experience of believing that we are flawed and therefore unworthy of love and belonging—something we've experienced, done, or failed to do makes us unworthy of connection." Many people confuse shame and guilt, but shame actually runs deeper than guilt and is much more toxic. Guilt is about something we've done, but shame is about who we are. If you felt guilty about lying to someone, you would think, *Lying is bad. I won't lie again.* Feeling shame, the thought sounds more like *I am a liar, and I am bad.*

For somebody with an eating disorder, a seeming solution to feeling bad about yourself is to do things to make yourself "good." Getting thin can sometimes be a symbolic gesture about becoming a worthwhile and lovable person—and this idea that thin is good is strongly reinforced by our culture. People with anorexia often find that once they get to their goal weight, they do not feel how they hoped they would, and so they set a new, lower goal weight. Other people with medium or higher weights feel bad about their bodies (feel bad about their *selves*) from the get-go. Other people feel that they are relentlessly chasing a thin body (a state of happiness) that they cannot achieve or sustain.

> "I thought once I reached my goal weight, everything would sort of fall into place, and I'd be happy, but I wasn't. So I set a lower goal weight, and a lower one and a lower one."
> —*Tieko, in recovery from anorexia*

> "When I binge, I get a break from thinking about my body."
> —*Christina, suffering from binge-eating disorder*

Numbing

The eating disorder can be a way to manage emotional chaos—it sort of narrows the field. If your emotional experience is profoundly negative, it's only natural to want to numb your feelings. People have a desire to numb all sorts of feelings, including anger, sadness, guilt, and shame. Even feelings that most of us would consider positive like connectedness and interdependency can feel threatening and seem like they need to be dulled.

Eating disorders do this in a number of ways. First, restriction, bingeing, and purging all activate brain chemicals that make you feel disconnected, spacey, and numb as a result of normal physiological processes. It is hard to feel anything except overwhelmingly hungry or full. Second, eating disorders take up a lot of headspace. If you're thinking about food and calories all the time, you don't have to think about other things. You don't have to think about how you feel, bad things that might have happened to you, whether or not you're good enough, or even the effects that the eating disorder might be having on your life.

"I'm always either eating, looking forward to eating, or regretting eating. Nothing else is on my radar screen. And sometimes I like it that way."
—*Connie, diagnosed with binge-eating disorder*

Control

For many people with eating disorders, life seems overwhelming and riddled with anxiety. Indeed, many things happen in life that are outside of our control, and for some people, such as trauma survivors, things have been extremely out of control in the past. People with eating disorders often feel that food is the one thing they can control. Even if they don't feel in control of anything else in life, at least they can be in charge of what goes into their body. Other people simply cannot make them eat or stop eating (you might have learned this the hard way, dear reader).

"Everything else is out of my hands, but nobody can make me eat."—*Jericho, struggling with anorexia*

Black-and-White Thinking

This is the idea that things are either all good or all bad. For someone with an eating disorder, black-and-white thinking applies heavily to food and bodies. Foods like desserts are totally bad, while foods like vegetables may be safer. A person is either thin or fat, and there may not be a lot of middle ground or a lot of appreciation for nuance and context. Black-and-white thinking may also apply to how people with an eating disorder think about themselves, their relationships, and their world as a whole. We all engage in black-and-white thinking at one time or another; it serves to reduce anxiety by making the world more manageable. Of course it has the immense drawback of keeping you from seeing shades of gray—and color!

> "It's always the extremes: all or nothing. I'm like that with everything."—*Jennifer, struggling with bulimia*

Perfectionism

Perfectionism is a lack of tolerance for perceived flaws. Perfectionism is often driven by shame and the idea that any flaw or vulnerability in the self would reveal a wholly bad and toxic person, which is a great example of black-and-white thinking. For example, if I have a small stain on my blouse, that will reveal me as a totally incompetent and disgusting person. If I have dishes in the sink when people come over, they will find out that I'm lazy and irresponsible. You can see here how shame goes hand in hand with black-and-white thinking to create perfectionism. If you can only be all good or all bad, and you can identify one bad thing about yourself, then you must be all bad. So in order to be good, you have to be perfect!

> "I'm so afraid of being lazy, I create this huge buffer by working so hard, all the time, at everything."
> —*John, struggling with orthorexia*

Competence and Effectiveness

Not all of the feelings that drive eating disorders are negative. Many people report that they get a sense of accomplishment out of their eating disorder, and feelings of achievement are an important human need. This takes on even more salience for people who have trouble feeling competent and effective elsewhere in their lives. I once worked with a man who had a doctorate but, due to some of his mental health difficulties, worked as a server at a local restaurant. We often discussed that without his anorexia, he wouldn't be sure if he'd be able to feel that he was good at anything.

> "I don't know what else I'm really good at, but I'm sure I'm good at my eating disorder. At least there I know I can win."
> —*Erin, diagnosed with anorexia*

Emotional Security

For people who have been engaging in disordered eating behaviors for some time, the eating disorder can become something to rely on. It provides a sense of comfort; it's steady and predictable. Many eating disorders are characterized by a sense of ritual: eating in a certain way, weighing in a certain way, even checking the body again and again to ensure that there is no weight gain. As burdensome as they can be, these behaviors often function to make people feel safe.

> "I don't know who I'd be if I didn't have my eating disorder, and that's scary."—*Miya, diagnosed with anorexia*

EXERCISE 10: Furthering Compassion

This writing exercise will help you identify more clearly with your partner's emotional experience. After all, the feelings that your partner is dealing with are universal; it's your partner's way of dealing with them that is different from yours. In your journal, write down times when you have had the following experiences:

A time you experienced shame

A time you numbed or wanted to numb your feelings

A time you felt out of control or a time when being in control was very important to you

A time you wanted or needed something to be perfect

A time you worried about your competence and effectiveness

A time when you needed emotional security

The Story Behind the Disorder

Gathering together all this information, the story behind the eating disorder begins to emerge. With empathic understanding you can begin to put your partner's emotions, history, and behavior together into a narrative. Here are some other stories that can help you imagine more clearly what life might feel like to your partner.

• *Anna's Story*

"I was always teased for being chubby when I was growing up. I lived in LA, so a lot of the people around me were very image conscious. It didn't help that my mom and my sister are really thin without even trying. I took after my dad, taller with a kind of pear shape. Everybody else in my family was always very busy with their social lives, so when I got home after school, I would go through the pantry and eat everything I could find. Looking forward to that got me through the day. So the teasing kept getting worse, and the eating kept getting worse. By the time I was in fifth grade, kids were calling me Chunks.

"Then in seventh grade, I got mono and I lost a ton of weight. People at school noticed, and they gave me lots of compliments. It seemed like all of a sudden people were being nice to me. In retrospect, they had probably just gotten more mature, or maybe they felt bad because I had been sick, but at the time it definitely seemed like it was because I was thinner. It felt great. I started really watching what I ate, just terrified that the pounds would pile back on.

"I had my first boyfriend a couple of years later, but we broke up when he started being interested in another girl. I was devastated, and I kept thinking that if only I were thinner, he would have wanted to stay with me. The problem was, I was already at a healthy weight. It was just that losing weight had done so much for me in the past that it had kind of become my go-to, especially when it came to trying to make myself more wanted and accepted.

"Of course, I realize now that this was the beginning of my eating disorder. It wasn't just that if I were thinner, I'd maybe not have lost my boyfriend. It was that if I just concentrated on being thin and nothing else, then I didn't have to feel anything. I only had to deal with getting thin. I didn't have to deal with how hurt I was or how rejected I felt. This became my way of dealing with my feelings for years afterward.

"Because it worked. People don't get that about eating disorders—you do it because it works. I felt powerful, on top of it. Other people were weak and lazy because they couldn't keep their weight in check, but I was in control. I was capable. Other people needed to eat all the time, but I didn't need anything. As time went on, I relied on my eating disorder more and more to make me feel this way. It became an obsession.

"By the time I was in college, my grades were really poor. I was out of it a lot of the time, from not eating. It seemed like the only thing I could do well was to be thin. I didn't really make any friends, because most of the social occasions were about eating and drinking. The school gym was open 24/7, so that felt like a place I could always go. I started taking laxatives whenever I felt fat, and eventually it didn't feel like my body would function properly without them.

"I met my husband, Charlie, at school; funny enough, he worked at the gym. But it's hard to be in a relationship while I have this other thing going on. He wants my time and attention, but I feel like if I don't give all of my time and attention to being thin, then I'll end up some fat slob, and this will all be for nothing. I know that's a sick way of thinking, but I can't get it out of my head."

• *Ben's Story*

"I started throwing up while I was wrestling in college to keep my weight down. I was a middleweight, but my coach said that I would do better as a welterweight. A few of the other guys were doing it too, and it really didn't seem like a big deal. After a little while, I started thinking *Well, if I'm just going to throw up anyway, why don't I just eat whatever I want?* I didn't know then that this wasn't a realistic way to control weight, and since I wasn't allowed to have any sort of fat or sugary foods in my house when I was growing up, this seemed like heaven to me.

"I started bingeing a lot, and it became more and more important. The whole thing feels really comforting, like the one indulgence I have in life. I have trouble relaxing any other way— when I sit down to watch a movie or something, I think, *This would be so much better if I had some food.* I've started doing it more frequently as my life has gotten more stressful—when I entered the work world, got more responsibilities, and especially when I became the boss.

"Before every binge, I go to the store and get all the foods I don't usually let myself eat: cakes, cookies, donuts, chips, and pretzels. I put on one of my favorite comedies and tear through everything I've bought. Sometimes I still feel like eating then, so I take stuff from the kitchen too. After, my stomach feels so full, it's like I'm going to burst. I go throw up four or five times in the bathroom—it feels like I'll never be comfortable unless I do. I know it's gross, but it seems like I just have to do it.

"My wife is so supportive of my trying to get better, but I feel really ashamed about what I do, so I don't talk about it much with her. I have been seeing a therapist, though, and I've started to realize a lot of the reasons that I binge and purge have to do with my feelings. It's hard for me to feel good about myself, and it's hard for me to relax."

EXERCISE 11: Do I Fully Understand My Partner's Story?

You can see from these stories how complex and multifaceted eating disorders are. They can be influenced by so many factors—the cultures we grew up in, our family and friends. They meet a lot of different emotional needs, and once they start, they cause their own emotional havoc. In your journal, respond to the prompts below to see if you fully understand the complexities involved in your partner's experience. If you have questions for your partner, hold on to them. The next couple of chapters will be talking about communication, and asking your partner questions about her story is a great place to start.

What factors contributed to my partner developing an eating disorder?

How did the eating disorder get entrenched?

What role do emotions play in my partner's eating behavior?

How does our culture affect my partner's eating disorder?

What role do friends and family play in my partner's eating disorder?

What role do I play in my partner's eating disorder?

What sorts of things make it easier or more difficult for my partner to deal with food?

Next Steps

Understanding your partner's story puts you on the path to approaching your partner in ways that are helpful and avoiding things that can be unhelpful. The most helpful approach isn't always obvious, though, even with a very deep understanding. Many seemingly helpful strategies fail to work, and it can be easy to fall into traps of relating in ways that are neither helpful nor healthy. The next chapter will review some of these common pitfalls, so you can avoid them!

CHAPTER 5

Getting Away from Negative Patterns of Relating

Having a deeper understanding for your partner's struggle will give you a clearer intuitive sense of what she needs from you. But it's actually pretty difficult to find just the right tone, and you are likely to make mistakes at first. In fact, it's easy to inadvertently make disordered eating behaviors more likely! Any strategy that increases your partner's anxiety will increase her likelihood of using the eating disorder to cope with that anxiety. Then, it's a good bet that your anxiety will go up as well, perhaps accompanied by disappointment or anger, and you'll be more likely to use unhelpful strategies. This vicious cycle can be difficult to get away from, as you can see in figure 2.

Figure 2: How Negative Patterns Reinforce Themselves

This chapter will review some mistakes that people commonly make when dealing with a loved one who has an eating disorder. If you have engaged in any of these behaviors, don't beat yourself up. Many of these approaches seem like they should work or sometimes do work, but only for a short while. In fact, many things you may do or say to be helpful are received in the opposite way from how you intended.

In this chapter, you'll learn to avoid the common mistakes partners make when communicating with their loved one—and what to do instead. Chapter 6 will delve more deeply into the topic of finding more healthy ways to relate.

Commenting on Weight, Appearance, or Food Choices

"I tried on this dress and I asked my boyfriend if he thought I looked fat. And he said no. And then I thought, *Oh, I look skinny? I wonder how much skinnier I could get. Maybe I'll skip lunch.* I know that's messed up, but it's just what went through my head."—*Alyssa, struggling with anorexia*

Many partners think that if they could just convince their loved one that she is beautiful or he is handsome enough already, the eating disorder would go away. This seems to make sense until you learn that eating disorders are only partially about outward appearance. Actually, even positive comments about appearance often have the opposite effect of what was intended! Any time that you are focused on weight or appearance, even in a positive way, the eating disorder has an opportunity. The words that you are saying get twisted until what your partner ends up hearing isn't what you meant at all. Until you know a lot about eating disorders, it is hard to see the harm in something as reassuring as saying "You look amazing!" But comments like these can have disastrous consequences for a person with an ED because they feed into the eating disorder in unexpected ways.

Think about the eating disorder like the world's worst (and meanest) translator. If you tell your partner that she is skinny enough, she hears, *Good job dieting (but I bet you can do better)!* If you mention that your recovering partner is looking healthier, she's likely to hear this as *You are starting to get fat.* If you say, "I think you're beautiful," your partner might hear *I think you're beautiful now, and looks are important to me or I wouldn't mention it. You better not get fat.*

I know, I know—that isn't what you meant at all. And when you meant well, it's totally unfair to have your words twisted this way. But no amount of arguing with the eating disorder translator is going to help, so it's better to avoid these comments completely.

Instead, keep your focus on your partner's inner self, who she really is. If you think that your partner is smart, funny, or kind, let her know about it! And let her know how important these things are to you. If you respect your partner's determination at a hobby, ability to multitask at home, or assertiveness at work, say so! A well-timed compliment that takes focus away from appearance can go a long way. In this way, you can bolster your partner's actual, real self—the person that you love—instead of superficial aspects of identity like body shape or size.

It can be a part of eating disorders to ask for reassurance a lot. This could have to do with certain foods or with body size and shape. At these times, it can be helpful to redirect focus on how your partner *feels* rather than the disordered eating concerns (looking fat, eating too much, and so on). You can say that you've learned that food-and-body concerns are often about much more than they seem at first, then ask if there are any deeper feelings your partner is experiencing. Leave up to your partner whether or not she wants to talk about it, but let her know that you're there for her if she does.

If your partner asks if a dress makes her look fat, you might want to reply by asking if she feels comfortable in it. Or you might want to see if she's asking because she's feeling anxious or upset and what you can do to help if that's the case. Ultimately, whether or not the dress makes your partner look fat is irrelevant. The real questions that drive eating disorders—*Am I good enough? Am I lovable? Am I at risk for being out of control?*—are more likely to be answered if you don't get sidetracked into a discussion about your partner's body. When somebody is seeking reassurance about their body or food, it's really a communication that the eating disorder is activated and that they need your support.

It's also always okay to decline to comment. If you need to, you can make me the bad guy here: "I've learned from that book I'm reading that it's better if I don't say anything about that, but I'm here to talk if you are struggling with ED stuff. How are you doing?" Rather than just saying, "I won't talk about that," this response opens up the conversation to the deeper feelings that might be happening.

Unhelpful Comments About Weight, Appearance, or Food	It Would Be More Helpful to Say
"You look great!" "It isn't attractive when you are so thin." "I'm so glad you're looking healthier." "Gee, that's a lot of calories."	"I love that T-shirt. It's such a great band." "I think you are smart, funny, and kind. I'm very attracted to those things about you." "I'm so glad you seem less anxious about food." "Gee, that looks delicious."

Bashing Your Own Body (or Someone Else's)

"My boyfriend always points out fat people on the street to try to show me I'm smaller than them, but all it does is make me panic about the idea of being fat. Yeah, maybe I'm not that fat now, but I could be. And that makes me really anxious."
—*Jeanine, struggling with bulimia*

The stay mum rule goes for commenting on your own and other people's appearance as well, especially making negative or disparaging comments about weight or food. These comments make the person with the eating disorder confused and angry—if you are willing to judge someone else's body or diet, it follows that you might judge your partner's as well. How can you tell your wife she needs to love her body as it is, and then make a nasty comment about what some stranger on the subway is eating? How can you try to get your boyfriend to stop obsessing over his weight when you are weighing yourself every day too? It's really helpful to embrace body-positive ways of thinking, both to be supportive and because it's honestly a healthier way to think about food-and-body issues. If this is tough for you to do, it might be a good idea to enlist the help of a professional.

Body Bashing	It Would Be More Helpful to Say
"I need to lose weight." "I hate my love handles." "Carly looks like she lost weight."	"I love my body at any size." "My body doesn't have to look one particular way. My health and happiness are what's most important." "Carly seems happy."

Being a Food Cop

> "When my boyfriend gets all over my case about what I've eaten, it makes it pretty tempting to just lie to him. I feel like I can't change what I'm doing, and I don't want him upset with me on top of it."—*Julia, diagnosed with anorexia*

One extremely common problem among partners of people with eating disorders is food policing. The food cop role can take many guises: asking your partner repeatedly what he has eaten, tracking his food, inquiring about his weight, or attempting to catch him being dishonest about food.

Here's a story about a couple who exemplified this problem and what helped them. Henrietta and Ralph were deeply in love and had a wonderful relationship. But as Ralph began to eat more and more, Henrietta began to worry quite a bit. Because women had always done the cooking in her family, she felt responsible for Ralph's eating behaviors. It didn't seem to her like he was taking any responsibility at all, so she tried to monitor and police Ralph's eating behaviors. She made elaborate, vegetable-based meals that took her hours to prepare, and then she took it personally and got extremely upset when Ralph opted for fast food instead.

She'd end up yelling at him that he didn't care about her or how it made her feel, and that she was just trying to make him be healthy. Ralph would end up feeling so guilty and angry that he'd go out and get fast food to numb his feelings. So the cycle continued, and the problem escalated. Henrietta's good intentions and hard work made Ralph feel worse, and Ralph's eating behavior made Henrietta feel like she needed to take more control of his food (and so on).

With lots of work in couples counseling, Henrietta saw that playing food cop wasn't working. What Ralph needed her to be was a caring wife, not a dietitian and not Julia Childs! She stopped watching everything Ralph ate and didn't grill him about it anymore. She still cooked, but her meals were less elaborate and she stopped taking it personally if Ralph didn't have as much as she expected, or if he ate other things in addition. As Ralph felt more supported and less criticized, and as he did his own work in therapy, eventually he was able to take more ownership over his food choices. Stopping the food cop mentality didn't solve the problem by itself, but it allowed the couple to start working on their dynamic, and both Ralph and Henrietta are now much happier.

Being a Food Cop	It Would Be More Helpful to Say
"Are you lying to me about eating?" "Are you sure you want to eat that?"	"I found out that you really didn't eat like you had said. If you're having a hard time, I'm here for you." "Sometimes that's a food choice that you make when you're stressed. Do you want to talk?"

Taking It Personally

"It makes it so much worse for me that my boyfriend thinks this is about him. Now I feel really guilty a lot of the time."
—*Steven, diagnosed with bulimia*

Although it has a huge impact on you, the eating disorder is not about you. Similarly, the various struggles and triumphs your partner encounters along the way are not about you. You cannot fix your partner. While this may seem harsh, it is actually quite liberating! Your partner doesn't have this eating disorder because you somehow fail to love her enough, communicate your love enough, or make her feel worthwhile. Your partner has the eating disorder because she has trouble doing those things for herself.

One client said he felt like it was a slap in the face when he found his wife's binge foods stashed away after he had been going to a great deal of trouble to drive her to dietitian appointments and eat healthily in front of her. It made him think she didn't care about everything he was doing. But when I spoke with his wife, she said that actually she appreciated everything her husband was doing quite a bit—she even felt guilty at times that he was doing so much. But having the binge foods available helped her feel safe, like she could have an emotional release valve if she really needed it. It didn't have anything to do with him. When he took it personally, it made her feel really guilty.

Mark, the husband in another couple, thought he had an ironclad case for taking it personally. His wife, Stephanie, only really binged and purged when she was angry with him. He often avoided conflict because he didn't want her to engage in symptoms.

But the problem here was not that Mark sometimes made his wife angry. Conflict is a normal part of every relationship, and it's actually a very healthy thing if you deal with it well. The problem was that Stephanie had trouble knowing what to do with her anger. In therapy, she worked to learn that it's okay to be angry, even at people you love, and she found healthier ways of expressing it. She and Mark communicate much better now, and although Stephanie sometimes still binges and purges when she gets angry, Mark knows that it isn't really about him. Because he isn't taking it personally, he's able to be much more supportive of Stephanie when she's feeling triggered.

Taking it Personally	It Would Be More Helpful to Say
"You aren't eating because you want to punish me for that argument." "You're throwing up the dinner that I worked so hard to make!"	"It seems like you're having trouble with your food. I know things are also a little rocky between us, but I do want to let you know I'm here if you need me." "What's going on right now that is making you want to purge? Do you need to talk?"

Pretending It Doesn't Affect You

"I asked my boyfriend to get out of my face about my bingeing, so now he doesn't say anything about it at all. That doesn't help either. I just wanted him to talk about it differently."
—*Jessica, struggling with binge-eating disorder*

The other side of this coin is pretending that your partner's eating disorder doesn't affect you at all. Of course you have feelings about your partner's eating disorder, and it's important to acknowledge them so that they don't eat away at you. The key here is to find a healthy middle ground, where you don't take ownership of your partner's food behaviors but you do understand and speak about the effect that they have on you and your relationship. The eating disorder is not about you, but it does affect you.

It isn't okay for your partner to take your food without replacing it, leave a mess when purging, or fail to meet family obligations because of his eating disorder. It's also not okay to have these actions be an entirely taboo topic. By the end of this book, you will be able to self-reflect to see how your partner's behaviors affect you, acknowledge this to your partner clearly yet compassionately, and know your own boundaries around your partner's ED so that you can respond both firmly and lovingly.

Pretending It Doesn't Affect You	It Would Be More Helpful to Say
"It has nothing to do with me if you choose not to eat." "I don't care if you throw up all your food."	"I feel worried when I see you pushing food around on your plate. I care about you; let me know if you need some help." "I've learned that throwing up on purpose can be really dangerous. I'm concerned about your health."

Making Light of It

"When I first told my now-wife about my eating disorder, she said, 'Oh gee, a problem where you're too fit and healthy! Wish I could get that!' I realize now that she said that because it was too hard for her to face the reality of how serious my anorexia was. But it was really devastating. You wish you could spend every minute worrying that you aren't thin enough?

That you'll never look the way you want, and then you'll never feel the way you want? Never feel like you're good enough for anything? I wouldn't wish this thing on my worst enemy."
—*Joshua, diagnosed with anorexia*

People often make light of a subject to ease the emotional tension surrounding it or because they haven't yet been educated about how serious something is. But when it comes to an eating disorder, making light of it does not strike the right chord. It will likely make your partner feel like you don't understand the depth of his struggle or how painful it is. This isn't to say that you can't ever use humor with your partner, but it's important for both people to be truly in on the joke and find it funny. Humor is a gamble that fails when you haven't correctly read your audience, and in this case you can't win.

Making Light of It	It Would Be More Helpful to Say
"I wish I could catch anorexia for a couple months!" "Do you have any dieting tips?"	Nothing at all. There is never an appropriate time to make light of an eating disorder. Nothing at all. There is never an appropriate time to make light of an eating disorder.

Oversimplifying

When you say I should just stop bingeing and purging since it's bad for me, I'm like, wow, this guy really doesn't get it."
—*Pat, dealing with bulimia*

When you oversimplify, you basically act as though the solutions to your partner's struggles should be simple. Of course, it seems to you as though by just eating, or by stopping eating, or by not throwing up, your partner could recover from her eating disorder. But the reality is that these behaviors are driven by extremely complex patterns of feelings and thoughts. Although it might look easy from the outside, it's extremely difficult to change disordered eating behaviors. When you offer pat solutions, it can make your partner feel like he isn't really understood.

Lisa's husband, Frank, did a lot of oversimplifying before we worked together. He couldn't wrap his head around the eating disorder: how could eating be so hard? Frank had overcome a lot of issues in his personal life mostly by, as he put it, "pulling myself up by my bootstraps." He didn't see why Lisa couldn't do the same. Lisa, for her part, had trouble communicating to Frank just what it was about eating certain foods that made her anxious. She would always say that she wasn't hungry or didn't feel like eating, whenever he asked about it. (Part of this, of course, was that he asked in an incredulous tone: "Surely you can't have a problem eating *that*?").

It drove him crazy. But, in couple's therapy, Frank and Lisa learned how to communicate more clearly and listen better. As time went by, Lisa felt more and more willing to be emotionally vulnerable with Frank. She talked about feeling inadequate, even worthless, and feeling like she needed the high that not eating gave her in order to feel okay. She eventually shared with him that she'd had a history of sexual abuse, and that when she wasn't eating it was easier for her not to think about what had happened. Once Frank stopped seeing her problem as simple, he became open to hearing it for what it really was.

Oversimplifying	It Would Be More Helpful to Say
"You just need to eat more." "What's so hard about not throwing up?"	"I don't know what it'll take for you to overcome your eating disorder, but I do think a professional could help, and I am here to support you as well." "I understand how hard it is for you to stop doing what you're doing, for a number of reasons. Let me know what I can do to help."

Trying to Convince

"If one more person tells me that you don't actually lose weight by purging, I am going to absolutely lose it! I already know that, of course…sort of. But I can't help feeling like it might help. And anyway, I can't stand the feeling of being so full."
—*Jeremiah, struggling with bulimia*

Remember our optical illusion exercise in chapter 4? Remember how the lines seemed like they were different lengths, and they would continue to seem different no matter what anyone told you? This is why you can't just use logic to convince your partner to change her behavior. Even if she believes you on a thinking level, the eating disorder just won't let her get there emotionally. With an eating disorder, completely illogical ideas can make perfect sense—they just *feel* true.

And on top of this, remember that it seems to your partner like the stakes are really high. Remember our discussion about self-worth, and how it can seem to someone with an eating disorder like her value as a human being rides on her food decisions? You are asking your partner to put a lot on the line when you are asking her to challenge her eating disorder. If you try really hard to convince her to stop, she might even end up digging in her heels or being dishonest about her food behavior. Plus, she will be more anxious as a result of the friction between you, so she is actually more likely to engage in ED behaviors.

When you're tempted to use logic to convince your partner not to engage in ED behaviors, try approaching her about her feelings instead. Opening up the space to talk about the difficult emotions associated with disordered eating behaviors can go a long way toward reducing them and simultaneously bring the two of you closer together.

Trying to Convince	It Would Be More Helpful to Say
"But that doesn't make any sense."	"I know that you see it that way, although I see it differently."
"The way you're eating is weird."	"You seem like you're having trouble with your food. Are you okay?"
"You're so thin! You don't need to lose weight."	
	Nothing. Never comment on weight.
"No, tomato sauce isn't actually that fattening, because a lot of it is water."	"I really do think it's okay for you to eat tomato sauce. I'm not a dietitian, so of course I'm not going to go into specific food science about it, but I'll support you if you want to challenge yourself by eating it."

Strong-Arming

"My wife gets angry when I eat certain things. She says it's because she cares about me, but it really makes me feel bad. I don't want to eat the way I do, but it's really hard for me to eat any other way. I know it's hard to understand, but it feels like I can't help it. Then when my wife is angry at me on top of it, it's like I'm totally alone in the world."
—*Adrian, diagnosed with OSFED*

Strong-arming is actually a common behavior among partners because the ED can be so infuriating. Strong-arming usually comes from a place of frustration. Often it is not a first response but one that happens after multiple other strategies have failed. Usually strong-arming takes the guise of "putting my foot down" or "not putting up with this nonsense any longer." It doesn't really feel like you are bullying your partner; it feels like you are taking a strong stance against the eating disorder. But unfortunately the eating disorder lives inside your partner, so you can't attack it in this way without attacking him.

Strong-arming makes disordered eating behaviors more likely by creating deeply negative feelings inside your partner. One particularly problematic type of strong-arming is the empty threat—giving your partner an ultimatum that you will do this or that unless he changes his behavior, and then not following through. Empty threats happen when you don't take the time to really think clearly about what your actual boundaries are or don't practice enough self-care to really stand by them. Empty threats undermine your credibility and make your partner have difficulty believing you when you assert a real, healthy boundary.

Strong-Arming	It Would Be More Helpful to Say
"That's stupid, I'm not going to plan our night out around your eating disorder. If you don't like what they have, just don't eat."	"Let's go someplace where we can both get something we'll enjoy." Or "What can we do to make the evening easier for you?"
"I'm throwing away the scale."	"I don't think all of this weighing is helping you, and I'm worried. If you need to talk, I'm here."
"I'm leaving you if you don't get treatment." (You don't really mean it, or you may mean it in the moment but you haven't thought it through.)	"I've thought about this a lot, and I just can't be in this relationship unless you get help." (You really have thought about it a lot, you do mean it, you really do need to leave the relationship if your partner does not get help, and you will.)

Nagging

"My husband calls me at work every day to ask if I've had lunch. At first I thought it was really sweet and supportive, but now it's getting to be a bit much. It stresses me out."—*Melanie, diagnosed with anorexia*

Nagging is using quantity over quality in your communication. How do you know when you're nagging versus just reminding your partner? One thing to consider is your tone. If you could be construed as being either whiny or cross, it's likely that you are nagging. If you must say something more than once, it's a good idea to at least acknowledge that that's what you are doing and tell your partner that nagging her is not your intent. If your partner perceives your tone as nagging, it may not matter what the textbook definition is. It may be time to switch tactics anyway.

Nagging	It Would Be More Helpful to Say
"Have you called the therapist yet?" "Just have some muffin. Just a bite? What about this other muffin? Oh, come on. Just a little bite?"	"I know we've talked about this before, and I just want to let you know I still think that treatment is a really good idea. If you want me to help you find someone, let me know." "I know muffins are a fear food for you, but I really think you're up to it. Would you like to try? No? Okay. If you change your mind, I'll do what I can to support you."

Guilt-Tripping

"My boyfriend has a drug problem. He is always saying that he'll stay clean if I eat. It seems like a sweet, helpful way for us both to heal. But the reality is that I have a lot of trouble eating, so I feel like I'm totally stuck; if I tell him that I'm struggling, he might go out and use drugs. But if I say everything's fine, then I'm lying."—*Michaela, dealing with anorexia*

Like strong-arming, guilt-tripping is a tactic that you would probably avoid using in other circumstances. The stubbornness of eating disorders and the weight of their consequences make many people willing to do almost anything to get their partner to stop. Guilt-tripping takes many guises. These include bargaining your own self-care in exchange for your partner's, inappropriately bringing parenting issues into the mix, becoming histrionic, or going on and on about the effect that the eating disorder has on you (note that this is different from telling your partner clearly and calmly once, twice, or even repeatedly, using the principles outlined in chapter 6).

One type of guilt-tripping that is commonly seen is pleading. Saying "please" or "for me" may seem like a good idea because you're using your relational capital to get your partner to engage in healthier eating behaviors. Unfortunately, however, pleading works only in the short term and, as a by-product, your partner will feel bad about himself or resentful of you for using emotional manipulation to get your way.

Guilt-Tripping	It Would Be More Helpful to Say
"If you don't purge today, I'll stay sober." "Don't you see how much pain it puts me in when you don't eat? If you loved me, you would do better." "If you keep eating like this, you won't be alive to see your daughter's wedding."	"I've stopped drinking or doing drugs for my own well-being. I know it's hard to make changes. I'm here to support you if you'd like." "It's hard to see you struggle so much because I care about you, and I know it's hard on you too. I'm here to help." "I worry about your health."

Enabling

"My husband used to stock my binge foods for me. At the time, he thought he was being helpful. But it made me much more likely to binge at times when if I had to go to the store I probably wouldn't have. When he started therapy, he realized that he was afraid I would leave him if I wasn't bingeing."
—*Jessie, diagnosed with binge-eating disorder*

Enabling means engaging in behaviors that make it easier or more comfortable for your partner to engage in the eating disorder. This often happens because it is so difficult to let your partner feel bad. You might sometimes go out of your way to appease the dictates of the eating disorder so that your partner doesn't feel anxious or overwhelmed. The problem here is that when you do this, you reinforce the idea that your partner isn't up to saying no to her disordered-eating thoughts. In the short term, your partner may feel better, but in the long term you're reinforcing the idea that the eating disorder is too strong to challenge—and accommodating the ED may make you resentful to boot.

Another common reason for enabling behaviors is that on some deep and maybe unconscious level, a partner may be worried about what would happen if their partner ever fully recovered from their eating disorder. I know this is difficult to acknowledge, but it truly happens all the time and as a result of very normal psychological processes. Change is always stressful. This includes a change that could be potentially as positive as your partner's recovery from the eating disorder. Some people fear on some level that their partner would leave them if they weren't sick. Some are concerned that their own behavior would be under more scrutiny or that the relationship would be uneven. They may get their own needs met by playing rescuer. There are many subtle reasons why people may be partly invested in their partner being sick and themselves being well by comparison. If there is any chance that forces such as these might cause you to engage in enabling, it would be a great idea to sit down with a therapist to sort some of it out.

I'm not saying that you should never make any accommodations based upon your partner's eating disorder; enabling is different from being considerate. For example, it's unreasonable to ask somebody who is having difficulty eating a carrot to sit down to a five-course meal. So how do you know when you're enabling or when you're just being considerate? One handy metric is your own feelings. If you are feeling helpless, resentful, or overburdened, it's worth considering the possibility that you are engaged in an enabling behavior.

Enabling	It Would Be More Helpful to Say
"If it bothers you when I eat dessert, I'll just stop even though I don't want to." "I went to three grocery stores to try to find the granola bars you eat."	"It's okay for us to eat different things." "They didn't have the bars you like at the local store, so it looks like you'll have to eat something else. I know that might make you anxious, and I'm here to talk about it if you'd like."

EXERCISE 12: Acknowledging Missteps and Learning from Mistakes

It can be helpful to reflect upon your past behavior as you look toward developing new ways of relating. In your journal, reflect upon some of the times that you have used the maladaptive tactics described in this chapter. What brought you to these tactics? What were the short-term and long-term effects for yourself, your partner, and your relationship?

- commenting on weight, appearance, or food choices
- bashing your own body (or someone else's)
- being a food cop
- taking your partner's eating disorder personally
- pretending it doesn't affect you
- making light of the eating disorder
- oversimplifying
- trying to convince
- strong-arming
- nagging
- guilt-tripping
- enabling

Remember not to use this exercise as a tool to beat yourself up. You are in a difficult position, and many people have made the same mistakes. Instead, it's important to have a clear understanding of what behaviors you want to be sure to avoid in the future.

Moving Forward

Now that you have chiseled away at some approaches that don't work, a picture of a more healthy and supportive stance is likely beginning to emerge. The next chapter will clarify what healthy relating looks like and how you can begin using it to help your partner battle his eating disorder.

CHAPTER 6

Establishing Healthy Ways of Relating

Many of the problems covered in chapter 5 can be alleviated through having better boundaries and clearer communication. In this chapter, you will learn how to establish effective boundaries, how to communicate so that you and your partner really understand each other, and how to find a supportive stance that will help your loved one fight the eating disorder.

Establishing Good Boundaries

Boundaries are about where you end and someone else begins—or vice versa! Healthy boundaries protect relationships by making clear what each member is—and is not—responsible for. Without good boundaries, guilt and resentment inevitably build up between people. With healthy boundaries, you are yourself and you allow other people to be themselves. You don't make yourself responsible for other people's behaviors, feelings, or thoughts, and you don't expect other people to be responsible for yours. You don't try to control others, but you don't allow yourself to be controlled either. Establishing an appropriately supportive tone naturally follows from having a clear sense of boundaries. Healthy boundaries are firm, but flexible. They do not yield to guilt and manipulation, but they might adapt to different circumstances—for example, the amount of emotional intimacy that would be appropriate for a couple on a first date would be different from that of the same couple on their twentieth wedding anniversary.

Rigid Boundaries

Problematic boundaries generally fall along two dimensions: too rigid or too loose. When boundaries are too rigid, you don't allow yourself to relate with other people, let them know things about you, or ask for help when appropriate. You prize your self-sufficiency above all else, even at the cost of sacrificing deep and meaningful relationships. Some signs of rigid boundaries might be:

- having trouble being close to other people

- having very few relationships

- having mostly superficial relationships

- feeling uncomfortable sharing your feelings with other people

- feeling uncomfortable when other people share their feelings with you

- not taking feedback

When a loved one has an eating disorder (or any problem), it is often difficult for people with rigid boundaries to offer enough support. It might make you feel really uncomfortable to talk about emotional topics, or you might have a lot of trouble knowing what to say. So the default position becomes disengaging and maybe even seeming disinterested. It isn't that you don't love your partner or that it doesn't matter to you that he's struggling—to the contrary, it's often so difficult for you to see your loved one in pain that you have trouble bearing it.

However, the cost of disengaging is high for both you and your partner. Your support is an integral part of your partner's healing. After all, this relationship is probably his closest one. If you feel your boundaries are rigid, consider how they might be affecting you and your partner and see what you can do to move into a more supportively engaged position.

Loose Boundaries

Loose boundaries can be a big problem for couples as well. People with loose boundaries have trouble distinguishing between their own responsibilities and the responsibilities of others. They generally take on too much: this includes not only obvious things, like doing things for other people when you'd rather not, but also emotional responsibility for others. People with loose boundaries often believe that it is their job to make sure that other people are feeling okay. Here are some signs of loose boundaries:

- feeling responsible for other people's feelings

- doing too much for other people

- monitoring what other people are doing

- sharing private information or emotional vulnerability with people you don't know very well

- doing things that you don't really want to do for others

- resenting other people

- not respecting your own or others' privacy

A person with healthy boundaries might think, *This person is upset. Is there anything I can do for him (without sacrificing my own sense of well-being)?* In the same situation, someone with loose boundaries is more apt to think *This person is upset, I must drop everything to try to fix it.* The problem for people with loose boundaries is that they end up doing things that they don't really want to do and things that get in the way of their own well-being. Therefore, they can't help but feel resentful in the long run. They may also feel guilty when they advocate for their own basic needs.

EXERCISE 13: What Kind of Boundaries Do You Have?

In your journal, rate the degree to which you agree with the following statements on a scale of 1 to 5, where 1 means you hardly ever do this and 5 means you always do this. Meet yourself with some self-compassion if you don't like what you discover. Think of this exercise as an opportunity to learn.

A. Healthy Boundaries	B. Loose Boundaries	C. Rigid Boundaries
I say no when I don't have the time or energy to do something.	*I often say yes when I really want to say no.*	*I say no out of principle: people shouldn't rely on me to do things they can do themselves.*
Other people are responsible for their own emotional well-being.	*I am responsible for other people's feelings.*	*I don't care that much about how other people feel.*
I think my own thoughts, which are somewhat influenced by the ideas of other people.	*I have a tendency to swallow other people's opinions wholesale.*	*I don't really listen to other people at all when forming my opinions about things.*
I value emotional closeness with others, but I also value feeling independent.	*I need to be extremely close with other people almost all of the time.*	*I don't like to be emotionally close.*
I trust other people some of the time, when I feel that they have deserved it.	*I trust other people extremely easily.*	*I generally don't trust others.*

If you rated most of the statements in column A as 4 or 5, congratulations! You seem to have a healthy sense of boundaries. This will protect your relationship from resentment and guide you toward decisions that allow you and your partner to be separate, yet connected. If you rated many statements in column B as 4 or 5, you (and your relationships) would probably benefit from you making your boundaries firmer. This will prevent guilt and resentment from building up. If column C received the most 4s and 5s, more flexibility and adaptiveness would probably be helpful. It's okay to let people in sometimes.

Healthy Food-and-Body Boundaries

Here's where the rubber really hits the road when it comes to eating disorders: establishing healthy food-and-body boundaries. Ultimately, your partner's food choices are her choices to make. You can and should express your concerns clearly and unambiguously and let your partner know how those food choices affect you (more on this later). But you can't make your partner change what she's doing and, as you saw in chapter 5, attempts to do so almost always backfire.

Apply the following rule to food situations: *You are in charge of you, and I am in charge of me, but I'll do what I can to support you if it's healthy for both of us.* If you cook together, don't go to great lengths to make a special meal for your partner apart from what everyone else is eating. But if your partner wants to make something different for herself, don't give her a hard time about it. If your partner takes your food, she should be responsible for replacing it. Sometimes it's helpful to reinforce this boundary by having separate foods or separate grocery budgets. But don't get overly rigid about this; it's nice to be willing to take your partner on a date every once in a while. If your partner chooses to purge in the bathroom, it is her job to make sure that it is usable and clean afterward. Try not to take it personally if your partner chooses to purge food that you have made; it's about her eating disorder, not about the food and not about you.

Likewise, what you choose to do with your body is your own business. At the same time, if it isn't too much of a burden, one way to be supportive is by trying to eat normally (that is, as most other people would), especially when you are in front of your partner. Hopefully you can eat normally without feeling resentful. If not, unless there is a medical reason, it might be worth investigating your own relationship to food with a professional.

Communicating Clearly

All the emotional centeredness and appropriate boundaries in the world won't matter unless you can convey this stance to your partner. Yet, as important as it is, we actually don't talk very much in our culture about how to communicate well. As a result, surprisingly few people learn to speak clearly and listen for understanding. The following communication strategies will help you hit the right tone, convey your intended meaning, and accurately hear what your partner is saying.

Timing Communications Well

Never ever discuss loaded topics during a meal, when your partner is about to eat, or when he's just eaten. Food situations make people with eating disorders extremely anxious, and you want to have your important conversations at a time that is as calm as possible. To that end, it can be helpful to remember the acronym HALT, which comes from the substance abuse field: don't pursue the conversation when either you or your partner is hungry, angry, lonely, or tired. Both of you should be in as centered and grounded a place as possible. Remember, you aren't a mind reader, so it's always a good idea to check with your partner if it's a good time to talk before forging ahead with your topic. You can simply ask, "I'd like to talk to you about something. Is this a good time?"

Using I-Statements

Just as important as what you say is what you will want to avoid saying. How do you feel when somebody starts a sentence with "you are being…" and then goes on to characterize something you did or said? The structure of the *you-statement* usually puts the listener on the defensive, because what you hear next is likely either a criticism or an assumption about your experience (or both). Instead, I recommend using the *I-statement*. The basic idea is that when you want to communicate how you are feeling, you focus on your own feelings. This ensures that you are only speaking for yourself, not your partner. Other people are likely to be receptive to I-statements—after all, who can argue with you about what your feelings are?

Using I-statements doesn't mean talking only about yourself, but it does mean that you're talking about experiences only from your perspective. A good I-statement would be "I am worried about your health when I don't see you eat much." If you are talking about something your partner is doing, try to keep your focus on the behavior instead of the person: "I feel upset when you miss dinner" or "I am sad that you are struggling so much." Keep in mind that I-statements are not accusations; they are a way of providing information to your partner about what is happening for you.

You-Statements	I-Statements
"You're killing yourself."	"I'm worried about your health."
"You lied to me and you betrayed me."	"I'm feeling angry that you lied about food."
"You ditch me at every meal."	"I feel lonely when you don't come to dinner."
"You don't care about how you're affecting me."	"I have a lot of feelings about the impact your eating disorder has."

Staying on Target

When two people are having a difficult conversation, there is often a pull to change the topic. You express concerns about your partner's eating, he feels anxious and retaliates by talking about your drinking. What do you do then?

Should you have a conversation about excessive drinking? Absolutely. Should you have it in the middle of a conversation about your partner's eating disorder? Absolutely not. When the conversation seems to be going astray, it can be helpful to say something to this effect: "I agree that what you're saying is an important conversation to have, and I'd be happy to talk about that with you at another time, but right now I really want to express how I am feeling about X."

On the other hand, if the conversation is getting heated or out of control, stop talking about it! You can always pick it up at another time.

Listening Well

Of course in addition to letting your partner know where you stand, you want to clearly understand where your partner is coming from. This is where *active listening skills* come in: with this way of listening, you aren't just sitting back and letting the words wash over you. You are fully engaged in the process of listening, working hard to make sure that what you think you're hearing is what your partner actually said. You are also making sure that your partner gets that you are truly listening—then she will feel closer to you and more willing to share vulnerable or intimate feelings.

There are a few skills involved in listening this way.

HAVE THE RIGHT GOAL

The point of listening is to understand. It is not to fix the problem that the person speaking has, even if that person is in distress. The person who is speaking might want help with solutions at another time, but this is not a time for problem solving. Without first using active listening skills to make sure you deeply understand what's going on, any attempt at problem solving will be doomed to failure.

ASK QUESTIONS

This seems rather obvious, but it's amazing how often we fail to ask questions or fail to ask the right questions at the right time. When you find you need clarification to really understand what your partner is saying, ask a short and directed question: "Was it you or was it Molly who went to the store?" But when you really want to know about your partner's mental life, be sure to ask lots of open-ended questions along the lines of "What is that like for you?" or "How are you doing?" This allows your partner to offer up the things that are really important to him, not just whatever piece of information you happen to ask for. You'll find you get a lot more out of open-ended questions than questions of the who-what-when-where variety. Remember that questions are intended to elicit more conversation, so they should expand upon the topic that is already under discussion rather than divert the flow to something else entirely.

LOOK LIKE YOU'RE LISTENING

Active listening isn't only about listening. It's also about conveying that you're listening by using gestures and an attentive attitude, so your partner sees that you're interested and invested in what she has to say. This sends the correct message to your partner and makes her more likely to want to talk with you. As a bonus, a good listening posture and attitude actually make you listen better. So sit up straight, maybe leaning in slightly toward your partner. Make eye contact and nod a lot to show that you are receiving what your partner is saying. Interject brief supporting statements like "Really?" or "Wow." When your partner feels that you are really paying attention, you will be surprised by how much more she has to say.

REPEAT BACK WHAT YOU THINK YOU'VE HEARD

This is probably the most important piece of active listening. After your partner has said something, repeat what you think to be the important parts back, using slightly different wording to make sure you've gotten it right. Start with "What I think I'm hearing you say is…" and follow up with "…is that right?" You may be amazed at how many times your partner responds, "No, not exactly" or "It's a little more like this." When you've hit the nail right on the head, great job! This is an opportunity to show your partner that you've really got it.

Helping Your Partner Fight the Eating Disorder

This next section will discuss how to be helpful to your partner in more specific ways: using good communication skills to bring up your concerns and discuss treatment, supporting your partner through difficult moments, and embracing healthy food-and-body philosophies so that your partner doesn't feel alone as she moves toward these ways of thinking in recovery.

Communicating Your Concerns

It's important to communicate your concerns, but talking to your partner about eating behaviors can seem really daunting. Take some time to prepare for the conversation mentally and emotionally. It may help to review all of the principles of good communication discussed in this chapter and write down some of the key points you want to address. Writing down your thoughts can help you stay organized and on point during your conversation. You may also want to practice the conversation with a trusted friend or a professional.

I find that it's best to bring up a difficult topic slowly. First acknowledge that you have something difficult to talk about, and then let your partner know that it has to do with his eating behaviors. Be as specific and supportive as you can. If possible, focus on the food behaviors rather than on any changes in weight or appearance that you may have noticed. The only situation in which is it okay to make a comment about your partner's body is if you haven't observed any unusual food behaviors but your partner's weight has changed drastically. In this case, you must use care and caution to avoid labeling with words like "thin" or "fat."

Use I-statements to express your concern and to tell your partner what you would like to have happen. Usually, this is when you would tell your partner that it would make you feel less worried if he would be willing to get some professional help or talk to his treatment team about what's going on. If you are suggesting that your partner seek help for the first time, it's good to have the phone number for some local eating disorder specialists or the National Eating Disorders Association hotline (see resources).

Here are some examples of good communication based on the previous guidelines.

Example 1: "I've got something to talk to you about. It's about food. It seems to me like sometimes you push your food around on your plate without eating, and I've noticed that you seem to check the calories of everything you have. I'm worried about this and I've learned that maybe these things might be elements of an eating disorder. I'd like to be really supportive of you if that is the case, and I'd also really like it if you would be willing to check in with a therapist to see if there might be an issue."

Example 2: "I'd like to check in with you about your eating. It might be really difficult to hear, but I've noticed that you go to the bathroom for a long time after meals, and I can hear you throw up while you're in there. I'm worried that you might have bulimia. I'm freaked out about this because I know it's very dangerous. Of course, I could be wrong, but I'd like to let you know that if that is the case, then I'm here for you and I'll support you while you get treatment."

Example 3: "Is it an okay time for us to have a conversation? It's about food. Our grocery bills have been really high lately. Is your binge-eating disorder active again?"

It isn't enough to talk about your partner's eating disorder once and then drop it. Set aside a regular time to talk about the eating disorder and its effect on your relationship. This will keep emotions from being bottled up for too long and keep you from waiting until it's too late to alleviate problems. Not every conversation has to be a heartfelt tearjerker; sometimes a little check-in is fine: "Hey, how were you doing during dinner tonight?" or "Oh, you need to buy jeans? Yikes, that could be a field day for your ED. Let me know if you need me around."

Expressing Confidence

For people to think about change, it's not enough to see that the change is important to make. They also need to believe in their ability to do it. Eating disorder recovery is very difficult; your partner needs to have confidence that she can deal with the logistics associated with finding help, withstand the anxiety associated with body changes, and handle the difficult emotions that come up when the eating disorder isn't a distraction, to name only a few challenges! It would be helpful for you to remind your partner that you believe in her competence and efficacy. You can remind her of difficult challenges that she's faced successfully in the past, or just simply a well-timed "I believe in you" can go quite a long way.

Giving Instrumental and Emotional Support

There are two types of support, and understanding their differences can help you know when to offer which kind. Instrumental support is tangible. It involves doing actual tasks that help make your partner's life easier. This could include grocery shopping, preparing meals, paying for treatment, offering rides to treatment, or providing child care to allow for treatment. Emotional support is just that—emotional. It's less about doing than about being—being available, being there, being empathic, being loving. People entering into recovery from an eating disorder need both these types of support. The task before them is immense, and instrumental support helps them manage their actual lives as they go about the process of healing. Emotional support reminds them that they matter and that all of this hard work is worth it.

Recognizing Triggers

A *trigger* is anything that initiates disordered-eating thoughts and feelings. Triggers are not the cause of the eating disorder, but they make the eating disorder rear its ugly head. A trigger could be almost anything, food related or not. Gloria is triggered whenever she sees her mother-in-law, whose criticisms about Gloria's parenting make her feel anxious. Steven, on the other hand, doesn't get triggered by certain people but does start getting a craving every time he passes the store where he used to buy his binge foods. Jeff is triggered whenever someone compliments him on his physique. Mirrors and scales are often big triggers. Triggers can also be internal, related to certain thoughts or to feelings such as anger and sadness.

EXERCISE 14: Understanding Your Partner's Triggers

Below is a list of common situations that many people with eating disorders find to be triggering. In your journal, reflect on which of these might be triggering for your partner:

- eating more than usual
- eating less than usual
- seeing an extremely thin person
- seeing a much larger person

- having attention called to their body

- mirrors

- being photographed

- looking at photographs of themselves

- wearing certain types of clothes

- being nude

- clothes shopping

- grocery shopping

- being weighed

- talking or hearing about weights or other body measurements

- magazines, blogs, or websites that promote diets

EXERCISE 15: Understanding Your Partner's Triggers, Part 2

Some things, like seeing a number on the scale that they feel uncomfortable with, would cause almost anyone with an eating disorder to be triggered. Others are entirely idiosyncratic and depend upon the person's particular emotional makeup and history. In your journal, take some time to write more about your partner's triggers as you understand them.

Are there certain foods that trigger your partner? What it is about those foods that is triggering?

Are there certain places that are likely to trigger your partner? If so, what are they?

What social situations trigger your partner?

Do certain people tend to trigger your partner? What is about the relationships with these people that is triggering?

What emotions does your partner find to be triggering? How do those feelings trigger your partner's ED?

Of course, you won't fully understand these triggers without an honest conversation with your partner. If your partner is open to discussing it, use the good communication strategies discussed earlier to make sure the conversation remains helpful.

You can use the information you've learned about your partner's triggers to know what to possibly avoid or, when a trigger is unavoidable, to know when your partner might be in need of extra support.

Prioritizing Feelings over Food

When your partner is triggered, you can help by prioritizing feelings over food. In other words, focus on the feelings that come up for your partner rather than on disordered eating behaviors. Take a second and think back to what you learned in chapter 4: what is your partner's eating disorder really about? Usually, the closer you get to a deep answer for this question, the further away you get from talking about food. You start talking about topics like love, belonging, and worth.

Sometimes your partner might tell you that she is feeling triggered, in which case you will want to ask what she needs from you. Sometimes there are other indications. Obsessing about food, weight, and the body is part of the eating disorder, so many people with EDs frequently ask their partners if what they are eating is too much, whether it is okay for them to eat particular food items, and the most dreaded question of all—"Do I look fat?" I encourage you not to entertain these questions, but to redirect the conversation to the powerful feelings that are likely driving them. Don't shut down the conversation, but do change it to become more productive and meaningful.

You can say something along the lines of "I've learned it's better for me not to answer these types of questions, and I know that's annoying. But are you feeling really anxious? What do you need?" or "Is your eating disorder piping up?" Instead of joining your partner in obsessing about food and body issues, gently try to turn the conversation to deeper topics. At first you may be met with some resistance, because getting your reassurance is a short-term method for reducing anxiety. But if you calmly and clearly hold your ground and cultivate a genuine curiosity in your partner's emotional experience, eventually she may be able to open up to you more.

If not, that's okay too. You can also go the other way and give support even if you have no idea what's going through your partner's mind. For example, if a certain meal or moment seems hard, it can be really helpful to be a distracting presence taking energy away from the anxiety. Maybe play a game of hangman with your partner or tell her a funny story that's unrelated to food while she gets through a difficult meal or experience.

Engaging Your Partner in Nonfood-Related Activities

Food takes up an absurd amount of time, space, and attention for your partner. One way to be supportive is to think about things to do that are not centered around food. If you are planning a birthday for your partner, for example, consider bowling instead of an evening at a restaurant. Having a little space away from the pressures of food can give your partner some breathing space to re-center before the next challenge. Of course, you can't avoid food-related issues completely; they are everywhere. The idea here is to find some fun activities where food is not the focus of attention. Here are some examples:

- bowling
- ice skating
- book club
- art classes
- dancing
- hiking

- kayaking
- movies
- theater
- museum trips
- historical tours
- art classes

Remember that for many people with eating disorders, drinking alcohol can be just as problematic as eating. For some people, the calories in alcohol seem unacceptable, and for others alcohol may represent a numbing strategy that is ultimately harmful. Clothes shopping can be a triggering experience for many people as well. Always pay attention to context and to your partner's particular experiences when choosing a nonfood-related activity for the two of you to enjoy.

Getting on the Same Page

When someone enters into eating disorder recovery, in many ways they have to occupy a much healthier headspace regarding food than the average person does. Our culture has a disordered relationship to food, called the *diet mentality* by many professionals, and so approaching food in a healthy way means being at odds with some very popular ideas in our culture. If you are able to embrace healthy ideas about food and bodies and to share this viewpoint with your partner, she will feel less alone and more validated in taking these new stances. She will feel like you get where she's coming from and back her up.

Whatever the theme or the intention, there is a good amount of evidence that diets do not work. Instead, diets—which abruptly reduce the amount of food your body has gotten used to—trigger the body to slow down metabolism to hold on to body fat. So most people who go on diets not only gain back whatever weight they lose but usually gain back *more*. The diet mentality goes far beyond actual diets, though. Ideas such as "thinner is better," "foods are good or bad," and "foods are punishments or rewards" are all problematic philosophies falling under the umbrella of the diet mentality.

Additionally, as a culture we have an immensely strained relationship with our own bodies. Women have made a social sport out of negative body talk, and men are peddled unrealistic standards such as six-pack abs and V-shaped torso. On top of this, most of the images that we view on a daily basis are Photoshopped beyond all similarity to the human form. To be truly supportive to your partner, it is important to fight hard against these toxic ideas. The following philosophies represent alternative healthier ways to think about food and bodies.

HEALTH AT EVERY SIZE

The *health at every size* philosophy promotes the idea that any size body can be healthy. The truth is that there are many healthy weights and that a person's healthy weight is largely determined by genetic predisposition. When the body is too far above or below this healthy weight, or *set weight*, it naturally tries to return to it by either increasing or decreasing the hunger cues. So if you are listening to your body, you will naturally drift toward the weight that your genetics have determined.

Set weight may or may not be related to the BMI, or body mass index, that every person has. Many medical professionals use BMI as a way to tell if somebody is within a healthy weight range, but actually this is totally misguided. The math that is used to determine the BMI is meant for population statistics (these fifty thousand people should be within this weight range on average) and not individual statistics (this particular individual person, with this genetic tendency, this bone structure, and this metabolism, should be within this weight range).

ALL FOODS FIT

The *all foods fit* philosophy counteracts the fear-based, disordered idea that certain foods are totally bad, wrong, and off-limits. Instead, this way of thinking encourages people to think of the place that every food could occupy in their diet. Desserts, rather than being banned, are eaten for enjoyment and social cohesion. And carbs, instead of being taboo, are appreciated for providing energy for essential functions like brain activity.

Along with rejecting the idea of good foods and bad foods, this philosophy rejects the idea of foods as punishment or reward. Someone might say, "I've eaten salads all day. I'm going to reward myself with ice cream!" But the problem with this is it gets in the way of knowing what your body really wants. The idea of ice cream becomes appealing just because it's seen as a reward, but what if your body really wants another salad? Or salmon? Or a burger? Alternatively, food can be used as a punishment: *I had a cheeseburger at lunch, so I must have quinoa for dinner.* This thought leaves no space for you to actually want quinoa, which can be delicious! The bottom line is to stop thinking of different foods as either punishments or rewards—they're best when embraced as part of a balanced diet.

INTUITIVE EATING

Intuitive eating is focused on listening to the cues your body gives such as hunger, fullness, and cravings. The idea is that if you eat what you truly want when you want it, your body can recalibrate to begin letting you know what it actually wants instead of always craving supposedly delicious, but forbidden, foods like fried foods and desserts. You eat when you're hungry and stop eating when you're full. You eat what your body needs most of the time. Flexibility is paramount here— sometimes you will have to eat what is convenient or when it's possible, and that's okay too. You trust your body to make up for any mistake you might make in eating. Intuitive eating allows people to experience more freedom with food and, when people feel that way, they actually fall into a way of eating that is healthier and more sustainable than any diet.

Soliciting Feedback from Your Partner

So you've established clear boundaries, begun communicating better, and learned how to help your partner fight the eating disorder. How do you know if you're doing all these things right? Well for one thing, you can always ask! Now that you know the principles of good communication, pick a time when there isn't anything stressful going on, and check in with your partner. You can say, "By the way, I've been working on approaching you differently surrounding food issues. How am I doing?" Be as open and nondefensive as possible to the feedback you receive.

Next Steps

The skills presented in this chapter are all difficult to learn, and it will take some time to do them just right. Be patient with yourself and keep applying the basic principles consistently, taking note of what seems to work and making adjustments as needed. A mistake is nothing but an opportunity to learn. If you are having lots of trouble implementing these ideas, it may be that something else is holding you back, and you may want to check in with a professional for additional support and guidance. The next chapter will talk about how to apply these general rules to specific food and body situations that you are likely to encounter.

CHAPTER 7

How to Respond in Real-Life Food Situations

Y ou've learned a great deal about having healthy boundaries, communicating clearly, and supporting your partner in fighting against the eating disorder. The next step is to adapt these concepts to the types of real-life food-and-body situations you encounter every day. This chapter presents several common scenarios for couples who are dealing with an eating disorder and suggests how to respond with strategies that work.

Common Scenarios

These scenarios highlight strategies that could be applied to many other food situations. Not every scenario may apply to your relationship, but I encourage you to read about how to respond in each case because you may be able to apply many of these strategies to other problems you encounter.

1. "My girlfriend denies that she has a problem and won't get treatment."

Eating disorders play mental tricks on you. It's possible that your partner doesn't know that her food behaviors are a problem, or she may have some inkling but not quite be up to making the change. (See chapter 10 on stages of change to get a clearer understanding of this phenomenon.) Understand that you cannot make your partner change her mind. Sometimes, in fact, the harder you try, the more entrenched she will become. This doesn't mean, though, that you should stop sharing your observations. Your partner needs to know how her behavior is impacting your relationship. Hold fast to what you have observed and what you are feeling, while allowing for the possibility that you could be mistaken.

Don't forget to use I-statements: "I understand that you don't think it's an issue, but I feel very scared for your health when I see you taking laxatives, and I think that you might have an eating disorder." Or "I know you disagree with me, but the way that you're eating really concerns me, and I want you to talk to a professional about it." (See chapter 6 for a more detailed discussion of communicating concerns.)

In the end, even if you've said what you have to say and held your ground, you cannot make your partner enter into treatment. Some partners make treatment a condition of remaining in the relationship, and this is one of few situations in which I would advocate for this type of tactic—*but only if you really mean it*. It's okay for there to be certain things that you need to remain in the relationship, and it's okay for treatment to be one of those things. But remember that an ultimatum only works if you prepared to follow through with the consequence; otherwise, it's strong-arming and it's likely to backfire and hurt your relationship.

If your partner will not be moved, then you face the difficult decision of whether you can be okay with things as they are or need to leave the relationship altogether. If you choose to stay, you will be dealing with your partner's ED, possibly for life. This is a legitimate decision if you make it with your eyes open.

2. "My husband hardly eats anything at mealtimes and hides food so I won't see it hasn't been eaten."

Your job is not to pressure your partner to eat but to help him to reduce his anxiety. Mealtimes are already a very difficult time for your partner;

the middle of a mealtime is not the time for expressing your overall concerns about the ED or sharing your feelings about it. Take some deep breaths to make sure you are calm and centered—anxious or angry people cannot help others calm down. Focus on your partner's feelings instead of the behavior: "It seems like you are having some trouble with the food, are you okay? Do you want to talk?"

Don't put pressure on your partner to finish right now or monitor every bite he takes. Instead, try to make mealtime as normal as possible. Many people with eating disorders are helped by moving the focus away from the food at mealtimes, so try to engage your partner in games like hangman or tic-tac-toe or tell him funny stories about your day. Later, you can share with your partner specifically what behaviors you have noticed and use I-statements to say how those behaviors made you feel. You can encourage your partner to enter into treatment or share about these behaviors with his treatment team.

3. "I often hear my wife throwing up in the bathroom after meals."

Again, during or immediately following a meal is not the time for a confrontation. At these times, it's fine to just ask your partner if she's okay and if there is anything that you can do to be helpful. Later, when you are both feeling fairly relaxed and there isn't a great deal of pressure, it's a good idea to let your partner know that you did hear her. At this point don't mince words: be clear about exactly what you think is going on. Remember to use I-statements to communicate concern: "I heard you throwing up after breakfast yesterday, and I'm worried. Do you need extra support?" Of course, it's important to be open to the possibility that you might be wrong, but don't get dragged into an argument about it if your partner denies having purged. If she does deny it, simply restate that you had been fairly clear that you heard her purging, but that of course it is always possible that you are mistaken. Let her know that you hope this is the case but if not, and she is struggling with ED symptoms, you would like to be helpful.

4. "My boyfriend lied about eating disorder behaviors."

It's likely that you are having very strong feelings about having discovered your partner's dishonesty. Wait until you have talked through these emotions with a friend, family member, or therapist before approaching your partner. When you do decide that it's a good time to talk, use I-statements to let him know how you feel about his dishonesty ("I feel betrayed when you don't tell me the truth about things" or "I feel shut out when you lie to me about struggling with your eating disorder"). Acknowledge that the eating disorder has played a role in your partner's behavior, but that he is still responsible for being honest and forthright with you.

5. "My wife eats her food strangely, sometimes cutting it up very small or sometimes mixing things together that don't go."

Sometimes people with eating disorders do unusual things with their food, known as *food rituals*, in order to reduce their anxiety about eating it. This might include mixing together unusual combinations so that the food is less pleasant to taste, cutting food into very small pieces, not allowing it to touch the lips, or eating it an unusual order (for example, eating taco meat separately from the shell). It's best to follow the rubric of acknowledging your partner's likely feelings without becoming overly invested in changing the behaviors. Don't make her feel like she's under a microscope, but don't feel like you have to pretend you haven't noticed. Say something nonintrusive like, "You doing okay?" and leave it at that. Later, you can let your partner know that you've noticed this behavior and ask what she needs from you in those situations.

6. "When my partner goes into binge mode, he steals my food in the middle of the night."

If your partner's behavior clearly has a direct impact on you, then it's important to address the behavior. It's important that your partner be responsible for any food that he has taken but that he not feel overly shamed and judged for having done so. Try to treat this situation similarly to how you would if your partner had taken your car and used up all the gas without filling it back up. You wouldn't read him the riot act, but you wouldn't just be okay with it, either, and you would certainly mention it. Any food that your partner needs to replace should come out of his individual food budget if he has one.

Sometimes food isn't explicitly yours or his, and this is a typical way of operating a household. When an eating disorder is present and these behaviors are surfacing, however, it may be important to establish some clearer boundaries. Sometimes it can be helpful for different members of the family to have designated shelves or cabinets for food items that are considered to be just for them. Of course, items like butter and sugar will always be considered family foods, and if your partner goes through any of these, he is responsible for replacing them as well.

7. "My girlfriend always compares her food to mine."

This situation is inevitable because part of the eating disorder is about making comparisons. People with EDs often have difficulty looking internally and listening to their bodies to see how much they should be eating, so they have a tendency to carefully observe what other people eat. Of course, as with many disordered-eating patterns of thinking, there is no way to win here. If your loved one perceives you as eating way more than her, she might feel contemptuous and judgmental of you (try not to take this personally; it's an eating disorder thing). By the same token, if it looks to her like you're eating less, she is likely to feel guilty, greedy, and fat.

My advice is not to engage in this at all. Above all, do not fall into the trap of arguing with your partner or trying to convince or use logic to influence her. Don't try to reason with your partner that you are having a smaller dinner because you had a larger lunch or that your food looks only like more than hers because of the way it is arranged on the plate. It's okay for different people to eat differently, within healthy parameters. Instead, acknowledge the feelings that are likely behind the comparison: "It seems like you're having trouble being okay with what you're eating. Is there anything I can do to help?" When possible, try to eat fairly normally in front of your partner to avoid this triggering event, but once the food is on your plate, changing your eating because of your partner's reaction is usually going too far.

8. "My husband is always asking me to approve of his food. He asks, 'Is this too much?' And, 'Would a normal person eat this?' I don't know how I'm supposed to answer."

It can sometimes be difficult for people with eating disorders to determine what an appropriate portion size is, and the idea of potentially eating too much is extremely anxiety provoking. So people with eating disorders tend to ask for others' opinions about food quite a bit. But answering

101

these types of questions can be a trap. It's hard to learn to trust your own perceptions about food while relying on outside perspectives. The truth is that you can't answer this question for your partner, because you don't know how hungry he is.

And what if this time the serving is fine, but the next time it's more than you would have eaten? It would be weird to then say nothing when you've already offered your input about previous meals, and your partner would likely be able to tell that you actually think there's something a little off about his meal. This can not only instill panic but also teach your partner that he can't trust his own perceptions. It would be much better to say "I think you'll be okay even if it's a little less or a little more." Healthy eating is flexible, and part of recovery is to overshoot and undershoot portion sizes at times but to trust your body to handle it.

9. "My spouse refuses to eat meals with the rest of the family."

Sometimes it's easier for people with eating disorders to eat alone. They may feel self-conscious about what or how much they eat, food rituals, or the process of chewing. At the same time, having meals together is important for many families and it helps to get children accustomed to healthy eating habits. If it bothers you that your spouse isn't joining you, have a conversation about it. Use I-statements to let her know that when she doesn't attend meals, you feel disconnected from her and lonely. See if she would be willing to join the family for part of the meal or for some conversation after mealtime is over. Perhaps participating in family meals can be a goal for treatment. As with many ED behaviors, you cannot force your partner to change, but you can let her know the effect that she is having on you and your relationship. (See chapter 9 about how to cope with the impact of EDs on the family.)

10. "My husband says he cannot have certain foods in the house. Should I go along with this?"

The short answer here is it depends. Someone who is struggling with binge-eating disorder asking not to have multiple cakes and ice creams available is different from someone who is struggling with anorexia telling you that having a loaf of bread in the cupboard is too tempting for him. A good rule of thumb is how inconvenient it would be for you to keep that food out of the house. If it would be terribly inconvenient, the food is likely a staple and the request is probably an unhealthy one. However, if it's not a problem for you to keep a particular food out of the house (and it wouldn't be a problem for the average person), then go ahead and stop stocking it so that you can support your partner more fully. If you are confused about which scenario is which, and your partner is in treatment, you can always ask his treatment providers.

11. "My partner spends lots of money on food, and we're in debt."

One of the most difficult things to tackle is when your partner's eating disorder gets in the way of you successfully running a household together. As always, I advocate for clear, open, and nonjudgmental communication. In an instance like this, I also recommend considering having separate budgets for foods, and this holds true whether or not you have combined incomes. If your partner's food budget needs to be higher than yours, that's okay if you balance the overall budget in a way that feels fair to both of you. Maybe you will get extra funds to devote to a hobby or another enterprise, or maybe your partner can identify another area where she can spend less. This approach sometimes doesn't seem fair at first, because your partner can't help her binge-eating behavior, but she is responsible for making sure that she contributes her fair share to the household and doesn't take more of its resources than she is due. Ultimately, this strategy treats your partner like a responsible adult, which can help her to feel more empowered.

12. "My fiancé asked me to hide the scale."

Hiding things from your partner, even if he asks you to do it, puts you in a very difficult position if he ever wants them back. Instead, why not get rid of the scale altogether? Most people are weighed at the doctor's office often enough to have an approximate idea of their weight, which is usually enough information to be able to make good decisions about food. Be prepared, though, that doctor's appointments will likely be triggering events for your partner because of the scale. Many people with eating disorders ask their doctors to use *blind weights*, where the person being weighed does not see the scale or hear the number, and if being weighed is a trigger, this may be something to recommend.

13. "My wife has so many clothes, they are spilling out of the closet. But she looks at them and says she doesn't have anything to wear."

People with eating disorders often have a fraught relationship with clothing. Consider that your partner may be telling the absolute truth when she says she doesn't have anything to wear: eating disorders can cause your weight to bounce up and down so frequently that it's difficult to have clothing of the appropriate size on hand. A further problem is actually feeling comfortable in your clothes, which can be next to impossible sometimes. I recommend that my ED patients have a default outfit, a comfortable set of appropriately sized clothing that is always clean and ready for a day like this.

I would recommend not giving your partner a hard time about having trouble getting dressed. If clothing is taking up so much space that there isn't any room left over for your things, have a conversation about putting some items into storage. Note that putting items away, even if just temporarily, will likely be somewhat triggering for your partner so weigh your desire for more space carefully against this possibility and be ready for some fallout. If your partner spends a lot of money on clothes, consider separate clothing budgets much as you might set up separate food budgets for somebody who buys a lot of groceries.

14. "My husband doesn't want me to talk to anyone about his eating disorder."

Mental health conditions are so stigmatized in our society that it can feel humiliating to have people know about it. Respect your partner's privacy and be very selective in choosing your confidants. However, it is absolutely vital that you have support. An eating disorder in your romantic relationship is too much to handle alone. Choose one or two close friends or family members and run them by your partner. They should be people who are in your life but not as much in his, such as friends from high school or college. If this isn't possible, enlist the help of a professional. Talking with a therapist can be extremely valuable. If your partner is not okay with even this possibility, it's important to establish a boundary and get yourself the support that you need.

15. "I want to go on a diet."

The bad news is that if you go on a diet, it is likely to be triggering to your partner. People with eating disorders often compare themselves to other people and feel resentful when others are allowed to do things that they aren't. The good news is that diets don't work and aren't good for you anyway, so not going on one will only help you avoid a futile and potentially harmful path. Of course it's okay to be conscious about what you're eating, but a much healthier goal would be to practice intuitive eating, listening to your body so you can eat when you are hungry and stop when you are full. Intuitive eating can help you achieve the ends that diets so often fail to reach—a truly healthy body and lifestyle. And since it's likely that this way of eating will be encouraged for your partner, your embrace of this eating philosophy will help him feel supported and validated.

16. "My girlfriend can't afford any treatment for her eating disorder."

With a little bit of hard work, there is often some way to get ED treatment covered. First, if your partner has any insurance, call to see what your policy will cover. If she doesn't have insurance, see if she might qualify for Medicaid. The rules for qualification are always changing, so even if your partner has been rejected in the past, it's worth trying again. Another possibility at the outpatient level of care is to go to a local training clinic (see chapter 10). If you don't know of any local centers in your area, do an Internet search under "community mental health."

If your partner would be best served by a higher level of care, many treatment centers offer scholarships for those who need treatment but can't afford it. Your partner can call the main number to find out if this is a possibility. Some not-for-profit organizations also provide treatment scholarships for those having difficulty affording help (see the resources page in the back of this book for more information).

17. "My partner is lying to his treatment team. He tells them he's eating normally, but that isn't true."

When you're considering what to do about a situation like this, the real answer is that it depends. It is possible to reach out to your partner's treatment team. Given privacy issues, the team won't be able to talk to you about your partner (and may not be able to even confirm or deny if your partner is a patient), but the team will likely listen to what you have to say.

The cost can be enormous, though. Your partner is likely to feel that you violated his trust and impinged upon his boundaries—and you have. So make sure that you have a very compelling reason before contacting your partner's care providers. If you believe that your partner's health is in imminent danger, through either extreme ED behaviors or suicidality, it's a good reason to call. If the issue is a smaller one, such as one skipped meal or a membership at the gym that didn't lapse like your partner had said it did, it may not be worth it. If safety is not paramount, talk to your partner about what is going on and let him know that you think telling the team is an important step. If an ED professional who is seeing your partner ever asks you something directly, though, don't hide the truth. Honesty will be helpful to your partner in the long run.

18. "My wife is feeling very nervous about the holidays this year."

Holidays, especially those that revolve around food, can be extremely triggering for people with eating disorders. This is doubly the case if you are going to be celebrating the holiday with people who are unsupportive or do not understand about eating disorders. A few words of advice: plan ahead, plan ahead, plan ahead. Have conversations about what specific situations might be triggering—from food triggers like huge meals or not having much available to other potential issues like talking about politics, mentioning failed relationships or missed opportunities, or seeing certain family members. It might even be helpful to create a special signal that your partner can use to let you know that she has been triggered. Then you can do whatever you are able to be supportive. Usually getting some space, physically or mentally, from the triggers is the best course of action.

Looking Ahead

Now that you have a solid grounding on how to handle many food situations, it's time to devote some attention to some other complex issues that you may experience as a partner of someone with an eating disorder. The next chapter looks at issues related to sex and intimacy. Remember that if you find yourself feeling overwhelmed as you go through these pages, it may be helpful to take breaks and to practice the self-care guidelines from chapter 3.

CHAPTER 8

Improving Your Sex and Intimate Life

Physical intimacy is one of the most complex experiences that we can have as human beings. It can be a source of immense joy and connectedness, but it is also often fraught with anxieties and insecurities. It comes as no surprise, then, that difficulties in intimate life are extremely common among couples who are dealing with an eating disorder. In one study that examined the sexual relationships of women with eating disorders, almost two-thirds of the participants reported lowered interest in sex, increased sexual anxiety, or other sexual issues (Pinheiro et al. 2010).

This issue can appear in a variety of ways: too little sex, unsatisfying sex, not enough physical touch, or not the right kinds of touch. For many couples, both nakedness and physical touch can be extremely anxiety producing. In many instances, tension may result if half of the couple is more interested in sex than the other. Although issues surrounding sex and intimacy can look different among couples, the unifying theme is the same: difficulty experiencing and sustaining sexual and physical connectedness that is free from the influence of shame, anxiety, and resentment.

This chapter will discuss the ways in which disordered eating creates problems in the bedroom and, by challenging how you think about and approach your intimacy, will offer new ways to address these issues that may help you and your partner begin to reconnect.

> "Jessica is always turning me down for sex. It's hard to get rejected so much, so I've stopped asking. Sometimes I feel like we are more roommates than spouses."—*Lance, partner*

> "Both Ben and I have gotten really weird about sex. He doesn't want me to see him naked, and honestly, as he's gotten sicker I start getting anxious about the possibility that seeing him naked would make me not want to have sex. I don't want him to be hurt."—*Brian, partner*

> "I wish that Jim and I could have a more sexually satisfying life, but I hardly ever feel like it. I'm exhausted."
> —*Tianna, suffering with bulimia*

Understanding How Eating Disorders Affect Sex

Libido, or the level of desire a person has for sex, can vary across contexts, throughout the lifetime, and between partners. How high or low someone's libido is depends on a number of biological and psychological factors. Couples rarely line up in terms of libido—what are the chances that you will end up in love with somebody who has the exact level of sexual desire that you do, at the same times, and in the same contexts? It's a long shot.

And matters are made much worse when an eating disorder enters the picture. Eating disorders can negatively affect libido both emotionally and biologically. Sexual desire is largely based upon chemicals in the brain and body, and having a very low or high body weight can decrease the production of these chemicals. So can poor nutrition, even if a person is at a healthy body weight. These same chemicals result in vaginal lubrication for women and, without them, sex can become uncomfortable or even painful. Problems with these chemicals in men can cause them to have difficulty maintaining erections. Feeling bad about your body can also make it difficult for people with eating disorders to have an uncomplicated relationship with sexuality.

In other words, there are lots of ways in which the eating disorder may decrease your partner's sexual desire. Conversely, sometimes people who have food issues can become compulsive about sex, wanting to have it a great deal but maybe not always for reasons that are healthy. If this is the case for your partner, the website for Sex and Love Addicts Anonymous offers resources that may be helpful. This chapter will focus on coping with the more common issue of lowered sexual desire.

Body Shame

"I can't stand the idea of anybody seeing me naked."
—*Adrienne, dealing with UFED*

"I can't get into sex when I think about my body at all."
—*Jessica, diagnosed with anorexia*

People with eating disorders often feel terrible about their bodies, and sexual activity is a breeding ground for shame and self-loathing. You are naked, you are touched, you are touched places where you aren't normally touched, and you are focused on the body. People who generally do not feel comfortable in their bodies *especially* do not feel comfortable in their bodies sexually. If you don't feel adequate or normal, feeling sexy can be a pretty far reach. Experiencing yourself as desirable is an integral part of feeling sexual, and you can't feel sexy when you are disgusted with yourself.

To address body shame, you need to remember that good sex is focused on how it feels, not how it looks. Many people think that reassuring their partners would be helpful—and it's only natural to think that hearing "You're so beautiful" or "I find you so sexy" would decrease body shame. But, in reality, too much of this type of talk often serves to re-center your partner's attention to his body from the outside in (how it looks) rather than paying attention to it from the inside out (how it feels).

Instead of lavishing your partner with compliments if she has a body shame issue during sex, it might help to assist her in reconnecting with the physical sensations that she's having. You can ask questions like "Does this feel good?" and "How would it feel for you if I did x or y?" Keep your partner's needs in mind as you ask about new positions (somebody who is uncomfortable with her stomach might prefer sex from behind, whereas somebody who has body shame about her rear end would definitely not). Ask your partner what body parts she feels most comfortable with you looking at and/or touching and concentrate on those areas as you and your partner ease into things. Sometimes the simplest solution can be the best: how about experimenting with closed eyes or even a blindfold?

> "We found that talking about how my girlfriend Sara feels about her body has made a big difference. I used to always stroke her thighs, and I didn't realize she kind of hated it, because she feels uncomfortable about her thighs. Then we went through a thing where I thought I should do it anyway because her thighs actually do look very attractive to me, and I thought that she'd feel better about them when she saw how into them I was. Now I know better, to just listen to what she says she feels comfortable with. Expanding Sara's comfort zone is not my job."—*Norm, partner*

Sexual Anxiety

"Ugh, I feel like as soon as it seems like sex is on the table, I start getting really worried about how it's going to go."
—*Janna, struggling with anorexia*

People can have anxiety about intimate encounters for lots of different reasons. Performance anxiety, or the fear that you will not be able to satisfy your partner, is very common. This is generally acknowledged as an issue for men, whose ability to have penetrative sex depends on their ability to sustain an erection, but it is often a problem for women as well. Both men and women want to please their partners sexually and are apt to have concerns about their ability to do so or about sexual encounters going poorly in other ways. There can also be anxiety connected to body shame.

In response to anxiety, couples may go in one of several directions. Some begin blaming each other, letting tension and resentment build until it no longer feels like you are on the same team. Other couples suffer through unenjoyable sex in the name of preserving a "healthy" relationship. And other couples avoid sex altogether. Once you begin to avoid sex, it can be very difficult to reinitiate. Asking for or initiating sex after a dry spell can make either member of the couple feel extremely vulnerable. But whether as a couple you are putting up with unenjoyable sex or avoiding sex altogether, this dynamic will get more firmly entrenched as time goes on unless you address it. Some of the tools this chapter will address, such as mindfulness, lowering the stakes, and having regular conversations, can go a long way toward lowering sexual anxiety.

Sexual Rejection

Sexual rejection and the fear of sexual rejection pose another layer of problematic experiences. Rejection, or just the expectation of rejection, brings up powerful feelings of uncertainty and insecurity. It's common to deal with these feelings by blaming each other, even without being fully conscious that you're doing it. Rather than suffer the deep, difficult-to-deal-with feelings about not being desirable (which translates in our culture as not lovable and good enough), the potentially rejected person sometimes deals in blame: "What's wrong with you that you don't seem interested in me?" Then the person who is perceived as rejecting becomes defensive, and a vicious cycle filled with tension and bitterness ensues. The space for sex to be a light, unencumbered, and fun-filled experience collapses. Another possibility is to create distance to protect yourself from shame, and lose your connection with your partner in the process.

The Snowball Effect of Negative Sexual Experiences

"Every time I start feeling turned on, I get angry almost right away because I know that Jill is going to say no."—*Sara, partner*

"When Kevin and I start fooling around, I start worrying *what if it doesn't go well?* I think about times in the past when he hasn't been able to keep it up or when I freaked out. Then I start wondering if we should even be together—isn't passion a really important part of a relationship?"—*Brianna, diagnosed with bulimia and partner to an individual with binge-eating disorder*

113

The least sexy thing in the world is the burden of previous sexual problems. If you've had a history of trouble in the bedroom, the weight of that knowledge looms heavy during every potential sexual encounter. Sex takes on much more meaning than is either helpful or appropriate. Instead of "Wouldn't a romp this morning be a fun thing?" the questions between you and your partner now become "Will our relationship be saved?" and "Can we be normal as a couple?"

Of course, these extremely anxiety-producing ideas do not make positive sexual encounters much more likely to happen. To the contrary, anxiety is the most powerful anti-aphrodisiac there is. It results in pressure to perform, pressure to make sure your body and your sex look a certain way, and even pressure to feel desirous and desirable. And pressure, of course, leads to more negative feelings. This can cause a vicious and ever-worsening cycle that is hard to break free of.

Restoring Intimacy

If you can see negative sexual experiences such as body shame, sexual anxiety, or sexual rejection beginning to snowball in your relationship, don't despair. The sections that follow will outline some ways to break free of these habits and reestablish a healthy intimate life.

Acknowledging the Problem and Letting Go of Blame

One of the most important things that you can do for your life in the bedroom is to address your sexuality *outside* of the bedroom. If there is room for regular conversations about sex when the stakes are comparatively low (that is, sexual activity is not on the table), then you can both be freer from anxiety in an actual sexual encounter.

These conversations should be planned ahead of time and take place when you are not likely to be interrupted and when you are both likely to be feeling centered. It should be okay for either member of the couple to cancel the talk if not feeling up to it, but a pattern of cancellations should be addressed. These conversations need to be honest and caring; review the communication principles in chapter 6 for a refresher in this area. Use I-statements, listen for understanding, and practice a nondefensive approach.

Talking about sex together can put you and your partner back on the same team by making it clear that this problem is both of yours to solve. The approach should be "me and you against this sexuality problem" rather than "me against you." It is possible that your partner's eating disorder lowers his level of sexual desire, and because of this, it can be tempting to place the blame in his lap. But, did your partner decide to have a lower sex drive? Probably not. Did he really want an eating disorder in the first place? Blaming your partner or yourself won't get you anywhere, but working together and thinking creatively for solutions will. Remember to include the topics of body shame, sexual anxiety, and sexual rejection in your conversations about sex.

> "I felt really anxious about talking about our sex life together, but once we started, it really helped. Now I feel like it's not so weird or abnormal to have sex issues, and we can deal with it together."—*Mariana, partner*

Lowering the Stakes of Encounters

Again, the more pressure there is on a sexual encounter, the more likely it is to go awry. There is so much pressure in our society to have a certain kind of sex life that most people don't actually have, and there are such negative ideas about what it means if sex isn't going well, that it's almost impossible to feel positively about things! Then people worry that if sex isn't going well, there must be something wrong with one of you or with your relationship as a whole, making matters much worse.

The reality, of course, is that sex is just one part of life for you to navigate together, like any other. Sometimes it goes poorly, and sometimes it goes well. If your sex life isn't stunning, it doesn't have to mean that your relationship is doomed. The more you can keep sex in its proper context, the more likely it will actually go well! In this way, sexual problems are like quicksand: the harder you try to escape, the more you sink; but if you can just relax, it becomes easier to find your way to freedom. Try to let go of the idea of sex as validation or proof that your relationship works. Move from "Can this sex and this relationship work between us?" to "Let's try to have some fun together and see what happens." This will make it much more likely that you will have fulfilling and satisfying sexual experiences.

"It feels a lot better to be able to laugh it off when sex doesn't go well."—*Tim, partner*

"I feel so relieved since Susan and I started treating sex like no big deal."—*Kierra, diagnosed with bulimia*

Obtaining Active Consent

If your partner's sex drive is limited, obviously she may not be that interested in sexual activity. This is not your partner's fault; it's just how the body works. I can guarantee you that she will be even less interested in sexual activity that feels obligatory—mostly done to please you, the partner. To avoid this common trap, it's important to make sure that active and sincere consent is obtained at every stage. This means checking in to ensure that your partner is both willing and excited to move toward the next level of sexual activity every time you want to up the ante.

Many people are surprised that really empowering your partner to say no actually makes her much more likely to say yes. Many times, partners feel reluctant to engage in even low-level sexual activity such as snuggling or kissing because they feel that they won't really be able to say no to any sexual requests that follow. Partners become much more likely to participate in sexuality if they feel that consenting to any piece of sexual action is not consenting to the whole kit and kaboodle. It may very well be the case that your partner feels like snuggling or kissing but not genital stimulation. Or she may be interested in oral sex but not penetrative sex. Empowering your partner to say no to going further, without encountering pushback or hurt feelings, will make it much more likely that she will engage in the sexual activities that she wants to participate in.

You may already feel that any sexual activity between you needs to be consensual and exciting for both of you, but have you clearly and explicitly communicated this stance to your partner? People often have ideas that may not line up to the reality of what their partner expects. If your partner thinks that you won't be okay with her hitting the brakes, your actual intentions won't get you very far. Make sure that you express your willingness to stop at any point of sexual activity, and express this willingness both during sexual activity and during your regular ongoing conversations about your sex life.

"I used to shut down DeShawn for kissing because I really didn't want to have sex. Now that he's been super clear that he won't be pushy about it, I kind of enjoy making out from time to time. Sometimes I actually get into the mood for sex, too."—*Catherine, partner*

Expanding Your Definition of Intimacy

"Lance and I aren't ready to start having sex again yet, but we make a point to cuddle up every night. It really makes me feel closer to him."—*Sara, partner and diagnosed with OSFED*

"It has made a big difference since we've learned in couples counseling all types of touching are important. I feel so much closer to my husband now."—*Jasmine, partner*

It is important to remember that sex and sexual touch are not the only intimate needs that people have. Caressing, cuddling, kissing, and holding are all forms of touch with profound differences in terms of the emotional and physical experience. These types of touch are all extremely important—at least as important as sex and particularly important if you aren't having very much sex. They serve to increase the level of oxytocin, a hormone known as the *love chemical* or *attachment hormone*. It is important to communicate openly and nonjudgmentally about engaging in enough intimate touch. Intimate touch also promotes emotional intimacy.

Emotional intimacy is a feeling of being close with another person, of understanding him and being understood by him. Emotional intimacy depends upon lots of factors: engaging in enough of and the right kinds of communication, empathy and understanding, shared experience, eye contact, nonsexual touch, sexual touch, and sex. People with eating disorders sometimes have difficulty with emotional intimacy. It may feel overwhelming or even threatening for some people to feel emotionally close. Remember, the eating disorder is not only about your partner's food or body but also about deep feelings of not being good enough, of needing to be perfect, or of needing to be in control. Emotional intimacy is at odds with many of these psychological needs.

The key to overcoming emotional intimacy issues is to determine the ways in which your partner is willing to be emotionally close and to engage him at that level. Sometimes people are more comfortable having emotionally intimate conversations while doing something else like driving or walking. Sometimes eye contact feels okay but physical touch does not, or vice versa. Because many people can view emotional intimacy as a threat, the person who is less comfortable with emotional intimacy gets to set the boundaries.

It is important, though, to have frequent check-ins to make sure that the boundaries are really where your partner needs them to be, rather than getting stuck by default and not reevaluated even as you and your partner heal and grow. This is part of the value of scheduling regular conversations.

"Andy has trouble with eye contact, but I've learned to lean into his strengths such as snuggling and caressing."—*Jessica, partner*

Using Mindfulness

One way for both parties in a couple to address difficulties with physical and emotional intimacy is to focus on being in the present moment through the practice of *mindfulness*—and since you're the one reading this book, I'll just focus on you here! According to renowned mindfulness expert Jon Kabat-Zinn (1994), mindfulness is "paying attention in a particular way: on purpose, in the present moment, and nonjudgmentally" (4). When you are mindfully in the moment, you aren't ruminating about the past and you aren't projecting forward into the future. Mindfulness also means suspending judgments and evaluations, focusing on how something *is* rather than ideas about how it *should be*. In mindful sex, this means a complete focus on sensations as they occur.

This part is especially critical for reducing sexual anxiety. In mindful sex, you let go of expectations and you become okay with however it goes. You don't think about how you are performing or stacking up, but instead you let the sensations wash over you with attention on what is going on in any given moment. It might seem selfish not to focus much on what is happening for your partner, but the reality is that you don't need to pay conscious attention for your body to pick up cues. In fact, anxiety and being in your head actually get in the way of being able to intuit what your partner might want in the moment. Paying attention to your own experience makes it more likely that you will be able to naturally follow your partner's cues without anxiety getting in the way.

EXERCISE 16: Mindful Body Scan

Here is a lower-stakes mindfulness practice that will prepare you to enter this state of mind in a sexual encounter. Find a quiet time when you will be free from distraction, lie down in a comfortable place, and let your breathing slow down. Then focus on what is happening in your body by scanning each body part. Begin in your feet and gradually moving up your body. Notice the sensations in your feet—whether they are warm, cold, tired, achy, relaxed—however they feel to you. Then do the same as you move on to your ankles, legs, stomach, arms, and finally your face and head. If your mind drifts at any point, gently bring it back to the body part you are noticing. When you've completed this scan, write in your journal about the sensations and experiences you found.

Mindful Sex

When it comes to sex, mindfulness usually means you actually aren't thinking all that much. Instead, mindful sex usually means suspending thinking just about altogether and focusing on the sensations in the body. You certainly want to avoid thinking about what you look like—a harmful habit known to sex therapists as *spectatoring*. Instead, you focus all of your attention on how you feel. You will find that the simplest sensation takes on profound layers of complexity and becomes really interesting once you put your full attention on it. When distracting thoughts come up—like wondering about performance, your body, or your to-do list—let them drift by and re-center yourself with a deep breath or a mantra such as "be here now." I would recommend not even looking forward to or thinking about orgasms. Instead, allow your focus to be fully in the present moment.

Mindfulness has a certain contagiousness to it, and when you start allowing yourself to be present in the moment, you may find that your partner becomes more mindful as well. Of course, it's best to have ongoing regular discussions with your partner about what is going on for you, including your intention to become more mindful during sexual activity. You can share that you are trying it for yourself and ask if your partner is interested in trying it too, but take care to avoid being pushy, because many people experience the pressure to overcome anxiety to be anxiety producing!

> "Mindfulness has made a really big difference for Stephan and me. It's much easier to enjoy the moment if I'm not paying attention to five billion different things at once, especially my anxiety."—*C.J., partner*

Sensate Focus

Many couples who have sexual difficulties benefit from sensate focus, a technique that reintroduces mindfulness into sex by going through a series of graduated steps. It is best to go through this process with a trained sex therapist who can help you navigate potential pitfalls and setbacks, but the gist of the program is that a couple begins to consciously and mindfully reengage in sexuality by taking turns touching each other with more touch allowed each time.

In the first stage, *nongenital sensate focus*, the couple focuses on taking turns touching one another, but touching any erogenous zones or having any sex is not allowed. The first session focuses on parts that are visible while wearing clothing, and after that you can add nonerogenous body zones (or so you previously thought!), such as legs, arms, and back. Finally more typically erogenous areas such as buttocks and chest can be added. This progression helps the couple reconnect with mindfulness and enjoy the process of sex rather than focus on penetration and orgasm. Each member of the couple tells the other in a noncritical way what sensations are most enjoyable.

The second stage, *genital sensate focus*, follows all of the principles from the first stage, such as turn taking, nonjudgmentally informing your partner of what is working, and refraining from sex, but also includes genital touching. The touching can progress from breasts and nipples, the areas around the genitals, and finally the genitals themselves.

Finally, the couple can engage in penetrative sex. Throughout, orgasms can happen but should never be the goal—rather, the couple focuses on enjoying the process together.

Working with a Sex Therapist

A sex therapist is someone who is specifically trained to help couples address sexuality issues. Sex therapists receive more training in dealing with sexuality than other types of couples counselors, and they consider sexuality to be their area of expertise. If problems in the bedroom are primary for you and your partner, and you find that you need additional support, I would recommend looking up sex therapists in your area.

The Special Case of Sexual Trauma

Sometimes people turn to disordered eating behaviors as a way to numb the overwhelming feelings associated with sexual trauma, take back control of the body, or try to reduce sexual appeal. If you or your partner is dealing with sexual trauma, I highly recommend working with a sex therapist.

Sexual trauma makes sex and intimacy take on a whole new meaning, often one associated with pain, degradation, and humiliation. Having sex with someone who has been sexually traumatized is an extremely delicate business. The guidelines for obtaining active consent take on a whole new dimension, and it is important to check in with your partner frequently to make sure he is feeling safe and willing to continue. Frequent and explicit conversations about your sex life become even more important. Sometimes people with sexual trauma don't realize until later that something has made them feel uncomfortable, so checking in after having sex is important. Triggers exist for sexual trauma, just as they do for eating disorders, and it will help to learn about your partner's sexual trauma triggers and avoid them as much as possible. Again, if sexual trauma is a part of the picture, a sex therapist can help you negotiate this very difficult terrain.

"It seemed like Jeannie was randomly freaking out during sex, but when we started talking about it more, she told me that actually if there is liquor on my breath when I approach her for sex, it really freaks her out, because the man who raped her had been drinking. I had no idea, and I never would have known if we weren't having those conversations."—*John, partner*

Conclusion

Eating disorders can have a profound impact on your sexual and intimate life. They may cause anxiety, body shame, and low sex drive. This can easily result in a vicious cycle of negative sexual experiences in which both members of the couple become at a loss for how to reconnect. Ways to deal with these effects include lowering the stakes of sex, communicating openly and frequently about sex, staying mindful during sex, and working with a sex therapist. It might not be easy at first, but don't let this keep you from trying. Reconnecting with your partner physically and emotionally can be one of the most satisfying experiences there is.

CHAPTER 9

Fertility, Pregnancy, and Protecting Your Kids

Eating disorders affect reproduction and parenting in a multitude of ways. There may be difficulty conceiving a child or, alternatively, there may be a greater risk for unplanned pregnancies. This chapter will discuss how to address fertility and pregnancy issues with an eating disorder as a part of the picture. Eating disorders make parenting more complicated as well, and this chapter will cover buffering against the potential risk for food issues that your child may carry as well as how to discuss your partner's ED with children.

Eating Disorders and Fertility

"My wife and I are having trouble conceiving because of her anorexia, even though she's been in recovery for two years now. The doctors said that isn't terribly uncommon."
—*Zachary, partner*

Eating disorders have important implications for fertility that you and your partner need to be aware of. Some people who have had eating disorders may have more difficulty conceiving than others; an estimated 18 percent of patients seen in fertility clinics have eating disorders (Miller 2016). But a seemingly opposite problem is also true: women with eating disorders have many more unintended pregnancies than women without eating disorders (Bulik et al. 2010).

Both of these problems are connected with the effect that an eating disorder can have on a woman's monthly period. Some women who do not have adequate nutrition have highly irregular periods and some stop getting their period altogether, a condition known as *ammenhoria*. Many women with anorexia suffer from ammenhoria. Women with other eating disorders are certainly not immune to menstrual irregularities, though. Approximately half of women with bulimia do not have regular periods, and overeating can cause hormonal problems as well (American Pregnancy Association 2015).

If a woman does not get her period, this typically means that she is not ovulating: the body is not releasing an egg to travel down the fallopian tube and potentially meet up with some sperm—a necessary step for pregnancy. This explains rather neatly why women who have eating disorders might have a more difficult time getting pregnant than other women. However, it is possible to ovulate without getting your period, and this is particularly likely to happen if your menstrual cycle is highly irregular. Many people don't know this, which accounts for the relatively high rate of unintended pregnancies among partners affected by disordered eating (Ward 2008). In other words, do not assume that your partner is infertile if she is missing her period. If you do not want to have children right now, it is necessary to use birth control, no matter what your partner's menstrual cycle is like.

Eating disorders can affect fertility in men too. Both very low and very high body weight have been shown to lower the sperm count. Additionally, malnutrition may result in sperm that are not properly shaped (poor *morphology*) or that have difficulty moving along in order to reach the egg (poor *motility*) (Vogel 2015). Any of these problems can result in difficulty conceiving. However, men with eating disorders can be fertile, so again it's important for couples who are not interested in conceiving to use some form of birth control.

Acknowledging Your Feelings and Avoiding Blame

"I'm really angry that Carrie was so careless with her body. I've wanted a child ever since I can remember, and now we won't be able to have one at least for a long time. But things have been improving since I started talking through these feelings with my therapist instead of taking them out on her."
—*Edward, partner*

If you want to have a child and are having difficulties conceiving that are related to your partner's eating disorder, you probably have very strong feelings about it. The desire to have a child can be powerful, and not being able to conceive may make you feel angry, lost, resentful, or even bitter. And because it seems on the face of it that your partner has control over his eating behaviors, it can be easy to dump these feelings on your partner and to forget that your partner did not choose to have an eating disorder. I would encourage you to keep in mind that excessive blame and negativity only keep the cycle going. If your partner feels blamed and unsupported, this will make him more—not less—likely to have disordered eating behaviors. Disordered eating behaviors, of course, make the possibility of conception less likely.

If you're struggling emotionally, talk with a therapist and supportive friends and family members about the feelings that fertility issues are bringing up for you. Review chapter 3 to make sure that you are taking good care of yourself. You might also benefit from an infertility support group; you can go online to find possibilities in your area or refer to the resources page at the back of this book.

Addressing Fertility Problems

There are lots of options today for couples having difficulty conceiving. Newer technologies in reproduction can make conception possible when it might not have been in the past. Some possibilities include intrauterine insemination (IUI), in which sperm that might have difficulty traveling are inserted at the top of the cervix, close to the egg, and in vitro fertilization (IVF), in which the egg is fertilized with sperm outside of the woman's body and then the fertilized egg is implanted in the uterus. Some people who do IVF also opt for ICSI, or intracytoplasmic sperm injection, in which the additional step is taken of directly injecting the sperm into the egg. This can be particularly helpful if there might be any problem with the sperm's ability to penetrate the egg.

It is important to mention here, though, that the body also needs to be able to sustain the pregnancy if conception should occur. Women with eating disorders who do not have adequate nutrition for conception may not be having adequate nutrition for carrying a child. Don't assume that your partner's eating behaviors will change once she becomes pregnant. These behaviors can be extremely entrenched and difficult to change, even if the stakes are quite high. Make sure that fertility providers are aware of your partner's eating disorder if you are having difficulty conceiving and choose to get outside help. The next section will cover some of the ways that eating disorders can complicate pregnancy and how pregnancy can trigger eating disorders.

Eating Disorders and Pregnancy

"My pregnancy was the most intense challenge to my recovery by far. I felt so uncomfortable in my body, and other people were always in my face about my weight."
—*Sara, in recovery from anorexia and bulimia*

"I couldn't stand watching my stomach grow bigger every day. One part of me knew that it was a wonderful thing to accommodate the new life growing inside of me. Another part was screaming, *No! you're going to be so fat!*"
—*Tara, diagnosed with anorexia*

Pregnancy can be a joyous and miraculous time, but it can also be extremely difficult as out-of-control hormones, body changes, and anxieties about parenting all intersect. Gaining weight is necessary for a healthy pregnancy—and is utterly terrifying for people with eating disorders. Even though it is very clearly the right thing to do from a logical standpoint, the eating disorder can still make a pregnant woman feel like gaining weight is very wrong. This results in a terrible bind and loads of anxiety.

There are lots of other potentially triggering aspects of pregnancy. Doctors can get extremely focused on gaining the "right" amount of weight, and there are sometimes so many doctors that it's hard to make sure each one is aware of an ED history. People sometimes touch your body without asking. It's common, especially in the first trimester, to be extremely nauseous and to need to vomit, which can be particularly problematic for those that have had a history of purging though vomiting. Pregnancy hormones naturally cause some food aversions, which can raise anxiety about eating and make it difficult for a pregnant woman with an ED history to find enough foods that she feels comfortable with. Problematic family dynamics become more intense as the family contemplates expanding, and you feel completely out of control.

It's likely that the pregnancy will be triggering even if the partner who struggles with eating is not the one carrying the child. Many of the challenges of pregnancy are not with the biological pregnancy itself but with the emotional and psychological implications of getting ready to add to the family and moving on to a new stage in life.

Risks of ED Behaviors During Pregnancy

It's important to take a clear look at the potential risks of ED behaviors during pregnancy and to consider how you might be able to address them. During pregnancy, the baby gets all of its nutritional needs met through the mother, and the mother is sharing all of her nutrition with the baby. There needs to be much more to go around than there used to be, and not having enough or the right kinds of nutrition poses significant risks. For example, folic acid is extremely critical for helping a baby's brain and spinal column develop. Iron ensures that both the mother and the baby's blood will be able to carry oxygen around the body—and is vitally important since during pregnancy a woman has 50 percent more blood than usual (Hytten 1985). Calcium, vitamin D, DHA, and iodine are extremely important, as well, to support the developing fetus (Morse 2012). Supplements will not be enough, either; most nutritional experts agree that nutritional needs have to be met through food.

A woman needs to gain weight during pregnancy—depending upon her weight prior to pregnancy, anywhere from fifteen to forty pounds (Centers for Disease Control and Prevention 2018). If a woman doesn't gain enough weight, she may have a baby with abnormally low birth weight. Low birth weight is associated with breathing problems, bleeding in the brain, heart irregularities, intestinal issues, jaundice, poor immune system functioning, and intellectual or developmental disabilities (Institute of Medicine 2007). Later in life, adults who had low birth weight as a baby are also at greater risk for diabetes, heart disease, high blood pressure, and obesity (Hong and Chung 2018).

Purging behaviors during pregnancy increase the risk for dehydration, chemical imbalances, and problems in the heart (National Eating Disorders Association 2018b). And when a pregnant mother's heart isn't functioning properly, her baby will not be able to get enough oxygenated blood. Binge-eating disorder is associated with high blood pressure and gestational diabetes during pregnancy.

> "Thank god my baby turned out okay. He was a low birth
> weight and I know it's because I had trouble eating enough."
> —*Jamie, struggling with anorexia*

Seeking Help

For all of these reasons and more, it is tremendously important to make sure that disordered eating behaviors are under control before intentionally conceiving. If, however, disordered eating behaviors are ongoing during pregnancy because of a relapse or for some other reason, help is available. It is very important to have an honest conversation with your obstetrician/gynecologist as well as a treatment team of eating disorder specialists about these struggles. In addition, a support group on the web called Lift the Shame might be of use (see resources).

> "I had no idea how triggering my pregnancy was going to be,
> but I got a lot of support from my therapist, my boyfriend,
> my friends, and my support group."
> —*Qwanna, in recovery from binge-eating disorder*

Protecting Your Children

A child of someone with an eating disorder is at greater risk for developing food issues than another child would be, because eating disorders are partially genetic. Additionally, children of people with eating disorders are often exposed to disordered eating behaviors within the home, which is another risk factor for developing eating problems. Children who have a tendency toward perfectionism, competitiveness, obsessing, rigidity, or impulsivity may be at additional risk (Robert-McComb, Wilson-Barlow, and Goodheart 2011).

Don't panic, though. There's a great deal that you can do to protect your child, and you have already started by getting educated about eating disorders. The remainder of this chapter will talk about providing your child with resiliency against the forces that promote eating disorders, modeling healthy food-and-body attitudes, spotting eating problems early and getting effective treatment to quickly address any problems that come up.

Promoting Emotional Resiliency

The most important things that you can do to protect your child against eating disorders have nothing to do with food. Rather, they are about working to ensure that your child feels validated and heard, safe and supported. These factors will promote *emotional resiliency*, a general ability to deal with the ups and downs of life without engaging in self-damaging behaviors.

Of course, many people who felt connected with their parents and appreciated for who they are also grow up to have eating problems. But when they do, they are much more likely to seek effective help quickly. They have been taught that they deserve to feel good about themselves and their world, and they will notice that the feelings created by the eating disorder are different from the way that they usually feel.

Here are some ways to build emotional resilience in your child:

PRACTICING SELF-CARE

To promote a sense of calm in your child, it's important to work hard to be calm and centered yourself. Taking good care of yourself will not only help you have the mental and emotional energy to be responsive and attuned to your children but will also teach your children by example that taking care of yourself is important. This will make your children more likely to take care of themselves throughout their lifetime. Self-care looks different at different times but it includes making sure that you are eating enough, sleeping enough, drinking enough water, spending time with friends, having time alone, and engaging in meaningful work. Review chapter 3 for a full discussion of self-care strategies.

FOSTERING CONSISTENCY

One of the best buffers against stress is a sense of consistency. Consistency can mean many things in this context; most important is your children's sense that you will predictably treat them with care, compassion, and warmth. You won't suddenly or randomly become angry, withdrawn, or rejecting. In a more mundane way, daily routines promote a sense of predictability in the world. Waking up at the same time every day, having meals and snacks on time, and going to bed consistently can help children establish a sense of rhythm and calm.

ALLOWING APPROPRIATE CONTROL

A sense of control is also important for children to have as a buffer against stress. This doesn't mean that they should feel like they are pretty much in charge of their own lives—in fact, a feeling of too much control can be quite anxiety producing for little people who haven't figured out how life should work just yet! Rather, I suggest the idea of promoting control within developmentally appropriate parameters—basically, letting your children have choices that are appropriate to their age.

For example, you know that your child has to get dressed for school or day care. If you have a toddler, you probably want to let her choose between two or three shirts appropriate to the occasion. You might give and older child guidelines about the basic type of clothes he'll need to wear—sweats on a gym day or something nice on picture day—but would leave up to the child what to wear within that category. You might let a teenager choose most of her own clothes to wear or to buy while shopping, barring the few things that may not be okay.

A related issue is *body autonomy*, which is the idea that you are in charge of your own body. This is particularly important for children who might be at greater risk for developing food-and-body issues. A healthy sense of this early in life can prevent the need to overcompensate and take total control of your body in an unhealthy way later on (by radically controlling your weight or food intake). You can promote body autonomy in your child by asking before doing things like brushing hair or taking off and putting on clothes. Another thing that helps children feel in charge of their bodies is letting them know it is always okay to say no to hugging or kissing people, even relatives.

BEING RESPONSIVE

To promote emotional resiliency in your child, unambiguously send the message that it is okay to come to you with problems. This is especially important if your child has a genetic predisposition toward potential problems. You can send this message both explicitly (saying "You can always come to me with any problems you have") and implicitly by being responsive, taking your child seriously, acting calmly concerned—but not overwhelmed—when there's a problem, listening well, and trying your best to be helpful without overstepping your bounds.

Be conscious about how you approach all types of problems, from your partner's eating disorder to schoolyard bullies to cars that won't start. The way that you approach small problems sets the stage for how your children will expect you to approach big problems—the types of things that you will really, really want them to talk to you about.

Modeling Healthy Food-and-Body Behaviors

Children pay less attention to what you say than what you do. If your partner has an eating disorder, chances are good that your children may see her engaging in unhealthy food behaviors, such as not eating when hungry or not stopping eating when full. Even if there are attempts to hide these behaviors, children are extremely perceptive. This makes it extra important for them to see *you* dealing with food in a healthy way. If they can observe one healthy approach to food at home, they can learn what it looks like and have the opportunity to emulate it later on in life.

Again, children are much more perceptive than we think, so model healthy habits both when you know your children are watching and when you think they aren't.

The most important component to a healthy relationship with food is a low level of anxiety about it. The idea here is that you care about and pay attention to food but you understand that food is only one important area of your life. You generally eat when you are hungry and stop when you are full, paying attention to both the nutritional aspects of food and how enjoyable it is (cost and convenience often likely play a role as well). You don't feel like you need to eat perfectly, though, because you're confident that your body will give you accurate signals about what it needs most of the time. You don't treat food as a reward or a punishment; eating is not about being good or bad but about giving your body the fuel it needs in as enjoyable a way as possible. Family meals are a good opportunity to not only to provide some quality time for the family to connect and communicate but also to show your children these healthy eating behaviors.

Your partner may not always be well enough to participate in family meals if his food anxiety or bizarre food behaviors make it difficult for everyone to focus on family interactions. If your partner's presence prevents the family from having a calm and relatively anxiety-free meal, it's okay to have your partner join for only part of the meal, even just a cup of decaf coffee afterward if that's all that he is up to at the moment. As your partner heals, being able to reengage in family meals may be an important goal of treatment.

It is also important to talk positively about your body and other people's bodies, focusing more on what bodies can do and less on how they appear. Again, it cannot be emphasized enough that children learn how to treat themselves largely based upon observing how you treat yourself. Small comments can have a big impact. Even saying "Boy, I really need to hit the gym" without adding "because my muscles need to be used and my body enjoys moving" can send the wrong message. It's important to avoid criticizing your own body or other people's bodies in front of your child. Likewise, it's important to avoid lavishing other people with compliments when they have lost weight or bulked up, because this emphasis on appearance sends the message that the way someone looks is of paramount importance.

Finally, it's especially important to talk positively about your child's body. Remember that children's bodies are intended to look all sorts of ways. Some kids are smaller. Some kids are bigger. Some have chunky cheeks. Weight during childhood does not necessarily predict adult weight. The more important truth to keep in mind is that an unhealthy relationship with food in childhood can become an unhealthy relationship with food in adulthood. Carrying much more weight than you would genetically be primed for can be one manifestation of that. However, your child's body type is not the primary determinant of your child's relationship to food—and you can help ensure that your child's relationship to food is a healthy one.

Go a step beyond refraining from criticizing your children to actually helping them generate positive feelings about their bodies. When they are younger, the head-shoulders-knees-and-toes game can be a great vehicle for this. Another great vehicle is recognizing the things their bodies allow them to do. As your kids age, you might want to pepper your interactions with comments like "Look how fast you can run!" or "Thanks for picking those apples. I could never have climbed up that tree like you did!" Remember that we're talking here about positive feelings toward the body, not how the body appears. So "Your body loves to move to music!" is a much better statement than "You are so pretty."

> "I knew my husband had issues about his body, but I didn't realize that I had my own issues until I really started paying attention to how negative I could be about my body as well. I'm glad I've started working on it before my daughter is old enough to pick up those attitudes."—*Riya, partner*

Teaching Healthy Food-and-Body Behaviors

Providing learning opportunities when your child actually interacts with food is extremely important. You can teach low anxiety by modeling calmness and centeredness when it comes to food. It's okay if your children eat a lot, and it's okay if they don't eat that much. Children know how much they need to have; it's adult meddling that can get in the way. Try to create opportunities for your children to have a fairly wide variety of foods, but don't pressure them unduly to eat things before they are ready for them. The more your children feel that they are in charge of their food, the more they will want to engage in eating in a healthy way.

Ellyn Satter, an expert at child and family nutrition, suggests considering a division or responsibility when it comes to food. You are responsible for what foods will be offered and when they will be offered, and your child is responsible for how much of the offered food to eat, even if that means none at all. Remember that all foods fit when it comes to your child, so provide lots of fruits and veggies, but make sure that it feels okay to eat desserts or sweets occasionally as well. Satter also advocates for structured meals and snacks rather than grabbing food on the go. This creates a space to really pay attention to what you are eating, which teaches your child to eat mindfully and with intention (Ellyn Satter Institute 2018).

Teaching Media Literacy

One of the main forces promoting eating disorders is our culture's disordered attitude toward food and bodies. You can provide a buffer against this force by educating your children about how images in the media are made and why they are done that way. Firstly, it's important to remember that the goal of any advertising is to sell you things. To do that, advertisers need to convince you that you are missing out on or are in need of something. That means they have to create a feeling of not being okay with the way you are.

Often, advertisers provide images of unattainably attractive people using their products as a subtle way to make you feel bad about yourself, and like you need something, and then—bam! Here's this product, which the advertisers are hoping that you, on an unconscious level, will decide you need in order to feel better about yourself. This process is fairly obvious when it comes to beauty products, but it applies to just about everything that's marketed to us, from cars to laptops. Talk with your children explicitly about this process, teaching them to see through the hype.

It's also important to talk with your children about what real bodies look like, and to be clear about the fact that the people in magazines and on TV are not realistic. They don't look that way in real life—camera tricks and Photoshop create images of bodies that often would never be biologically possible. Children are exposed to approximately three thousand ads per day; even if they are media literate, this affects them on an unconscious level (Goodman 1999). So make sure you are talking about this subject often and explicitly.

EXERCISE 17: Envisioning the Parent You Want to Be

In your journal, reflect upon the way that you want to approach parenting, given all that you have learned. What sorts of things really matter? Is there anything that you wish you were doing differently?

Making Mistakes and Getting Support

Of course, no parent is perfect, and no parenting is without its moment of *I really wish that had gone differently*. The idea here is to hit the mark most of the time and not to make parenting mistakes bigger or more anxiety ridden than they have to be. It's always okay to get help from other parents, professionals such as parenting coaches and child therapists, or organizations such as your child's school or your religious community.

> "My daughter started having some body image issues last year, but because of all the work I've put into our relationship, she felt comfortable telling me about it. I got her some help right away, and now she's doing okay."—*Enrico, partner and father*

Spotting Food Issues

Given that your children may be at greater risk for developing eating issues, it makes sense to be particularly vigilant about spotting any food issues that may arise. Do not allow this vigilance to stray into the realm of paranoia, though, but remember that a calm and reasoned attitude toward food is an important protective force. With that in mind, here is a list of potential signs that a child may be having food issues:

- avoiding meals

- hiding food

- stashing food away

- lying about food

- becoming extremely picky (some pickiness is normal in children)

- losing or gaining lots of weight

- not growing as expected

- following rigid regimens such as the keto diet or the paleo diet

- speaking negatively about his or her body

- speaking negatively about other people's bodies

- becoming angry over food issues

- eating extremely quickly or slowly

- excusing themselves to the bathroom immediately after eating

- exercising or playing sports even when injured

- experiencing menstrual abnormalities

- socially isolating

If you spot any of the above warning signs, I would encourage you to approach your child for more information. Keep your conversation developmentally appropriate, geared toward your child's age. A teenager would be able to hear that you are concerned about disordered eating, but talking to younger children, you might want to just ask if certain foods make them feel bad or if they feel bad about their body. If you are unsure about whether something's going on, it is always okay to consult with a professional. Research shows that treating the issue early on is much more effective than working on something that has already become an established problem (Treasure and Russell 2011). An eating disorders psychotherapist who works with children or adolescents should be able to put you in touch with a dietitian and other team members as needed (for more information about team members, see chapter 10).

Disagreements About Feeding Children

It isn't uncommon for people with eating disorders to be unclear about what's an appropriate and healthy way to feed children. The eating disorder tells them, in no uncertain terms, that the disordered way of thinking about food keeps them safe. And who doesn't want their children to be safe? Remember, too, that with an eating disorder the stakes feel really high if you eat the "wrong" way: you will be not only fat but also unlovable and morally reprehensible. What parent wouldn't want to spare her child this sort of a future? While of course you do not want to indulge this type of thinking when it comes to your child's actual nutrition, it's helpful to understand where your partner might be coming from.

When you have conversations about feeding your children with your partner, it will be helpful to convey that you understand her good intentions. Be sure to have these conversations out of earshot of your children, at a time when both you and your partner are feeling calm. Review the guidelines for effective communication in chapter 6 before you begin, because any conversation that could be perceived as critical of your partner's child-rearing has the potential to go very much awry. Positioning the problem as being the ED, not your partner, will decrease defensiveness and keep the two of you on the same team. If your partner will not agree with your view of how to feed your child, see if she will agree to a consultation with an independent third party such as an ED professional or a reputable child dietitian. Sometimes hearing something from an impartial third party can be helpful.

Talking About Your Partner's Eating Disorder

When discussing your partner's eating disorder with your children, it is important to do so in a way that is loving and supportive of both your children and your partner. Try to convey a sense of calm reassurance. You can be clear that your partner is having a problem with food—so your children understand that those behaviors are not normal or typical—while also calmly reassuring your children that things are going to be okay and that your family will be focused on getting your partner the help he needs.

If your partner has not yet acknowledged the disordered nature of his eating, you may be able to avoid battles by using I-statements to speak about your own experience without having a direct confrontation about food or fighting about it in front of your children: "Dad doesn't want to eat dinner tonight, but I think that this fish is really good" or "I think it's okay to have two servings." Your children will not benefit if you engage in a lot of blaming or talking down to your partner in an attempt to keep your children away from eating issues—to the contrary, your children will likely get the message that it isn't okay to have problems or to be up-front about them.

Again, it's important to keep conversations developmentally appropriate. Children of different ages can handle different amounts of information, and telling children more than is really necessary about your partner's eating disorder will place undue anxieties upon them. When in doubt, go for the simplest and most concrete explanations possible: "Mom is having some trouble with food" or "Dad is working on his eating." Answer questions honestly but plainly, without giving additional details unless your child asks for them.

Conclusion

Eating disorders affect all stages of parenting. Fertility and pregnancy become more problematic, and children of parents with eating disorders are at somewhat greater risk for developing EDs. There is a great deal that you can do to protect your children, though. Making sure that they feel loved for who they are is a good start for any child. Showing them appropriate food behaviors and body attitudes can provide buffering against developing issues, and remaining vigilant about catching problems early on can ensure appropriate treatment if any problems do arise.

CHAPTER 10

Recovery over Time

Recovery is not simple. You can't just pick a day on the calendar to get over your eating disorder. It's a long process, with switchbacks and detours all along the way. It's also a very individual process; one person's recovery looks very different from another's. Sometimes recovery moves in leaps and bounds. Other times it may look more like two steps forward and one step back. This chapter will explore what recovery from an eating disorder may look like for you and your partner and how you might get there. We'll demystify many of the acronyms and technical terms you may hear along the way, and you'll learn about readiness for change, different treatment providers, and treatment types and levels.

Defining Recovery

"My recovery began the day that I stopped throwing up. I won't ever consider myself just recovered and done with it, though, because I am going to have to battle with this every day of my life."—*Erica, in recovery from bulimia*

"I consider myself recovered. I have good and bad days, like anybody, of course, but I don't worry about my body the way that I used to. It doesn't take over all of my headspace, and

I generally treat my body really well. And I treat myself well too."—*Samantha, previously diagnosed with anorexia*

Different people define recovery differently. Some people believe that you can never fully recover from an eating disorder because someone who has had an eating disorder always needs to be mindful about avoiding damaging behaviors such as diets or fasts (a good idea for all of us). Some consider recovery to start when you've stopped disordered eating behaviors, and others define recovery as freedom from fear of food and fat (along with an absence of ED behaviors). For some people, recovery means reestablishing a sense of worth and reconnecting with emotions. A more complex definition of recovery may mean being recovered from an eating disorder in some ways but not others. Remember that eating disorders are multifaceted, and so recovery is likely to be multifaceted too. My recommendation is to ask your partner what recovery means to him, and adopt the same definition.

EXERCISE 18: Understanding Your Partner's Definition of Recovery

Understanding how your partner defines recovery will put you on the same page about where your partner is hopefully headed. Asking these questions can also help your partner clarify exactly what goal she is trying to reach. Using the communication skills from chapter 6, ask your partner some of the following questions. In your journal, reflect upon your partner's answer to each question and what your partner feels recovery looks like.

1. Do you believe that a person can be fully recovered from an eating disorder?

2. How do you define recovery for yourself?

3. What is important to you in your recovery?

The most important thing to understand about recovery is that it is a process. A stint at a residential facility or a few sessions with a therapist is not enough to overcome an eating disorder. It takes a long time, often years, of concentrated effort. But with effective help and support, freedom from the eating disorder is possible.

Understanding Change

Given the complexity of recovery, it can be helpful for you to think of the recovery process in terms of stages of change. This idea actually applies to many types of change that people make in their lives. However ready someone is to change their behavior determines the stage of change they're in, whether it is the precontemplation, contemplation, preparation, action, or maintenance stage (Norcross, Krebs, and Prochaska 2011). Examining stages of change in terms of recovery from an eating disorder can help you meet your loved one where he is, because different stages require different strategies for helping.

People in recovery typically don't simply progress through stages of change one after another. Rather they may skip stages, go backward, or even repeat sequences of stages several times. The important thing is to be able to identify what stage of change your partner may be in and to approach him based upon that understanding.

The Precontemplation Stage

"I don't have an eating disorder. I just like my food a certain way. Actually most of America has a huge problem with food, and I don't. I'm not overweight or eating tons of sugar like most people do. I don't even eat gluten."
—*Jim, in the precontemplation stage of anorexia recovery*

"I love my eating disorder; I can't imagine life without it. I feel like I'm totally in control, on top of the world."
—*Rhianna, in the precontemplation stage of OSFED recovery*

People in the precontemplation stage of recovery from an ED are not ready to change, and may not even be ready to acknowledge that there's a problem. They might make excuses for their eating behaviors, saying that concerned friends and family are overreacting and that their eating behaviors aren't really that bad, or even that they don't mind having an eating disorder. They are quite simply not ready to see that their eating may be a problem for them. This makes perfect sense in a way; the eating disorder is fulfilling an important emotional function, and people in this stage of change are not clear on how to meet that need another way. Would you want to give up your only way of feeling safe and in control in the world? Probably not.

Pushing a person in the precontemplative stage toward action is likely to be counterproductive. At the same time, it's important to acknowledge the very real effects that the eating disorder has on your partner, your relationship, and you. Focus on helping your partner weigh the pros and cons of her behavior as it is, for her and for your relationship. Share your concerns, often and consistently, even as you acknowledge to your partner that the decision to change is up to her. Considering that your partner might not be willing to change her behavior at this stage, you may also need to think long and hard about whether you are okay with remaining in this relationship if nothing changes.

The Contemplation Stage

"My eating disorder makes me feel powerful and in control. Sometimes, though, I feel like I am actually powerless when I want to do something, but my eating disorder just won't let me, like go out to dinner with my boyfriend at a place that doesn't publish their calories online."
—*Kaliah, in the contemplation stage of anorexia recovery*

"I love being thin and getting compliments, and I feel like I'm made to wear the most high-end clothes. I'm not sure whether it's worth being hungry and tired all the time, though. Some days I feel like it is, because I get so much back, and some days I feel like it isn't, because I have to give so much."
—*Jessica, in the contemplation stage of anorexia recovery*

In the contemplation stage, people go back and forth about whether or not to change. At one minute, they may decide that it would be best for them to get away from their eating disorder, but at the next they are back in its grip. Again, remember that the eating disorder does something for your partner: it solves some emotional problem and makes the world more manageable. Of course it will be hard to give that up, and deciding to change will be difficult.

During the contemplation stage of change, what your partner needs from you is to know that you understand his position. You can see that the ED does something for him, but you also see that it takes a lot from him too. One of the most important things that you can say to someone in this stage is "I get it. You are in a really tough spot. There are lots of reasons to change, and lots of reasons not to change. On the one hand, it would be scary and hard to let go of the eating disorder. On the other, it is causing the following problems..."

When your partner feels that you understand both sides of his ambivalence it becomes much easier to think about what it would be like if things were different.

The Preparation Stage

"I'm going to stop counting calories next month. I'm excited, but so nervous too!"—*Zania, in the preparation stage of OSFED recovery*

"I am almost ready to let go of hating my body."
—*Steve, in the preparation stage of bulimia recovery*

People in the preparation stage of change have decided that the current situation needs to change, but they haven't taken action just yet. A smoker in the preparation stage would have stocked up on the nicotine patch, outlined a rewards system for not smoking, and told people not to offer cigarettes after a certain date. But they would not have stopped smoking yet.

During this stage of ED recovery, your partner would benefit most from your expressed confidence in her ability to make the change. Change is hard, and she may doubt her ability to give up the eating disorder, handle the stress that might accompany the behavior change, and address all of the feelings that are likely to come up once the eating disorder is no longer a prime distraction. Letting your partner know that you believe in her ability to do all of these things can help her believe in herself too.

The Action Stage

"I am approaching food way differently than I ever have before."
—*Sam, in the action stage of recovery from binge-eating disorder*

During the action stage of recovery, your partner starts making changes to his eating behaviors. This change might be accompanied by body changes as well, which will be very scary for your partner. He may need reassurance that these changes are normal. During this stage, he will also need a good deal of instrumental support. Handling things at home while your partner is in treatment, navigating the insurance maze, and fielding questions from family and friends will free up your partner to focus on getting well.

The Maintenance Stage

"I've been in recovery for a while, and I feel pretty good about it. My therapist says the important thing now is to be careful about getting too complacent and not challenging myself."
—*Aloria, in the maintenance stage of bulimia recovery*

The maintenance stage of recovery is where people solidify the change that they've made into a new way of living. Some say that maintenance is the most important stage of change because it makes the change a part of your everyday life. It is important to remain vigilant during this process: eating disorders are sneaky, and your partner needs to continue to be surrounded by positive influences. During this stage, you will want to check in with their partner from time to time about how she is doing. It's also important to celebrate your partner's successes and to let her know how proud you are of her!

EXERCISE 19: Your Partner's Stage of Change

In your journal, make a note of what stage of change it seems like your partner is currently in. What does that mean about the best way for you to approach your partner?

Understanding Relapses

You understand by now that people don't just progress forward through the stages of change but often get stuck, repeat cycles, or go backward. This is all to be expected. A *relapse*, when a person in recovery returns to the eating disorder for a significant period of time or in a significant way, may happen for many reasons: an illness, a major life stressor, or even a positive change like a new job or a new house could be a triggering event. A relapse can actually be an important part of recovery by pointing where understanding or healing may have been incomplete in the first stages of treatment. Maybe a significant relationship was left unexamined, a traumatic experience was not processed, or not enough support was put into place. A relapse is like recovery saying, "Hey, you missed a spot!"

> "I had several really significant relapses before I finally entered into a more stable recovery. I'd be doing fine for a few months and then doing terrible for a few months—back and forth. I thought I was never going to get out."
> —*Ben, diagnosed with binge-eating disorder*

> "I had a really bad relapse a couple of years ago and had to go back into treatment. It made me realize that I hadn't really addressed my relationship with my parents the first time around, and now I feel more grounded in my recovery than I had been before."—*Tiwani, struggling with anorexia*

Seeking Treatment

As you and your partner investigate treatment options, several factors may affect what you choose. How entrenched the eating disorder is, how far your partner may have to travel to receive treatment, other responsibilities, and your financial resources all factor in decision making. Generally speaking, though, it is usually best to get the most intensive care that is available and that you can afford. Early and aggressive treatment is the most important predictor of success. I often meet with patients who are initially reluctant to take time off from school or work or away from the family to work on their health and who later report that doing so was one of the most worthwhile things they have done.

Treatment Levels

Since the eating disorder often goes back and forth several times before it is fully dealt with, it isn't uncommon at all for people to return to varying levels of treatment several times throughout the course of their recovery. It is important to note that returning to treatment more than once does not signal a failure but rather is an opportunity for the recovering person to reengage with recovery in a deeper or more meaningful way.

INPATIENT CARE

Inpatient care, usually in a hospital setting, is intended for those whose eating disorders have rendered them medically unstable. A doctor will recommend inpatient care at the point where it could actually be dangerous to attempt recovery without medical guidance. Often this is the situation when somebody has become severely malnourished and is at risk of *refeeding syndrome*, a condition caused by feeding the body too quickly after a prolonged period of restriction. Dehydration and electrolyte imbalances often lead to inpatient treatment as well. If possible, it is best to be at a hospital with a unit dedicated specifically to helping people with eating disorders regain medical stability. At this stage of treatment, the focus is not as much on understanding the deep roots of the eating disorder as on correcting the physical damage that has been done.

RESIDENTIAL CARE

At the residential level of care, people stay at a facility to engage in fairly intensive treatment for ED, consisting of therapy and set routines around food and mealtimes, but they do not require intensive medical care. Residential care can be helpful in several different ways. The break from work and family responsibilities allows people to really focus on getting better, and less choice over food allows them to nourish their bodies with less guilt and anxiety. Treatment at residential facilities generally includes group psychotherapy, individual psychotherapy, and family psychotherapy. Clients usually begin on fairly structured meal plans and slowly develop more and more choice over their eating while they get better. Meals at this level of care are generally well supervised, as the eating disorder often has a strong hold on people when they first arrive. Residential care also provides therapeutic meal support, a period of time to talk about the feelings and thoughts that a meal has brought up. The lengths of stay at residential facilities vary and are usually dictated by both a person's improvement and what the insurance company is willing to cover, as it can be fairly expensive without insurance support.

PARTIAL HOSPITALIZATION PROGRAM (DAY TREATMENT)

A partial hospitalization program (PHP), or day treatment, basically consists of engaging in treatment as though it were your job. You go in the morning around nine o'clock and generally come back home at around five. Typically, day treatments provide breakfast and lunch and the attendant therapeutic support. There will likely be one or two group therapy sessions during the day. Some PHPs provide individual and family psychotherapy. Participants usually attend two to three groups per day. Insurance plans generally cover PHP treatments.

INTENSIVE OUTPATIENT PROGRAM

Intensive outpatient programs (IOPs) are less intensive than PHP programs but more intensive than outpatient care (see next section). IOPs usually consist of three to four evenings per week, providing dinner and therapeutic meal support. Usually there's a psychotherapy group meeting after dinner in which the members can process what happened for them during the meal. IOP is generally covered by insurance.

OUTPATIENT

Outpatient care is appropriate once people can generally eat well enough to support adequate nutrition without meal supervision and support. At this level of care, the emphasis is on understanding the eating disorder more deeply and challenging some of the eating disorder's previous rules, such as never eating dessert or not eating after a certain time. Outpatient treatment should consist of a team including a psychotherapist and a dietitian, among others, a topic that is covered later in this chapter.

Types of Treatment

In addition to happening at different levels, treatment for eating disorders comes in a variety of different types. Here are some of the most common.

GROUP PSYCHOTHERAPY

Group psychotherapy for EDs generally falls into two broad categories: support-based psychotherapy groups and process-based psychotherapy groups. In support groups, members share common ground, celebrate each other's triumphs, and work on problem solving when group members hit sticking points. Contact outside of meetings is usually encouraged. In process-based psychotherapy groups, the point is to experience the intense emotions that can be brought about when you authentically connect with other people. Generally, process group members are advised not to be in contact outside of meetings. Group therapy may be found at any level of care but is most common in residential, IOP, and PHP programs.

Individual Psychotherapy

There are probably as many types of individual psychotherapy as there are therapists. Integrative psychotherapists, who draw on methods from several different perspectives, are often the most helpful for eating disorders, because EDs are so complex and multifaceted in nature.

Below are some common psychotherapy approaches that might be appropriate for you or your partner:

- *Humanistic psychotherapy:* This type of therapy prioritizes authenticity and genuineness, based on the belief that all people have the innate tendency toward growth. The therapist's job is to help remove obstacles toward that goal.

- *Cognitive behavioral therapy (CBT):* In this model, the therapist helps people examine and challenge the way that they are thinking and behaving. The idea is that what we think or believe affects what we do, and vice versa. Treatment is very active, and homework is assigned after each session.

- *Dialectical behavior therapy (DBT):* This type of treatment works with an approach that both validates and accepts where people are right now and challenges them to do things differently. DBT also provides skills for dealing with a variety of issues such as managing overwhelming feelings and being assertive with others.

- *Psychodynamic and psychoanalytic psychotherapy:* These psychotherapy methods aim to help people understand how unconscious forces, typically stemming from early relationships, affect how you function in the present.

- *Acceptance and commitment therapy (ACT):* This type of therapy helps people focus on what they most value in life and whether or not their actions are aligned with these ideals. It includes a focus on acceptance, or letting go of controlling things that can't be controlled.

Approaches can vary among therapists, and so can personality. Everyone is different. Some people need a straight-talking psychotherapist to cut through the BS and tell them what's what, and some people really just need to be accepted and understood for who they are. Gender and age may make a difference as well. It's a good idea to interview several therapists before choosing one to make sure that you have the right fit.

COUPLES COUNSELING

Couples counseling can play an integral part in treatment and, in my opinion, is one of the most important, most overlooked treatment modalities available. After all, your romantic partner is often your closest relationship in life, and the health of a romantic relationship is a tremendous factor in the health of both individuals involved in it. Without support, it may be very difficult to implement all of the new ways of relating to your partner that are discussed in this book, and a professional can help you anticipate pitfalls and setbacks that might be particular to you as a couple. To find a couples therapist, I recommend going to the website for *Psychology Today* and searching for your zip code; you can also ask your partner's providers for recommendations.

BODY-BASED TREATMENTS

Body-based treatments can be extremely healing for eating disorders—after all, the fundamental problem is the relationship with the body. Body-based treatment might include yoga, tai chi, or acupuncture. Body-based treatments should take place within the larger context of multiple modes of healing, and while providers do not need to specialize in eating disorders, it is important that they have some sense of what is appropriate for someone with an eating disorder (not to comment on weight or size, and so forth).

MEDICATION

Sometimes medication is a part of treatment. Medications might target depression or anxiety, because these conditions often drive disordered eating behaviors. Other medications can directly address food cravings or stimulate appetite. Medication alone is not likely to be helpful because disordered eating is so complex, but as an addition to a comprehensive care plan it can sometimes be invaluable. Note that once started, medication should be discontinued only under the guidance of a psychiatrist. With some medications, suddenly stopping can be extremely dangerous.

FOOD-BASED TREATMENTS

Food-based treatments are where the rubber hits the road for eating disorders. These interventions help people receive adequate nutrition and restore a healthy relationship with food. What follows are some of the more common types of food-based treatments.

Feeding tubes. If people are really struggling to feed themselves even minimally, they may be given a feeding tube for a period of time. A feeding tube goes in through the mouth or nose and supplies nutrition directly into the stomach. Sometimes a feeding tube makes early recovery easier for people by removing the issues of eating for a short period of time, allowing them to focus on fighting the eating disorder mentally. It also ensures that a person will be getting enough nutrition to allow the brain to function properly, obviously an important component of any successful treatment.

Therapeutic meal support. Therapeutic meal support is one of the most valuable treatments available for eating disorders. This is because it takes place at the moment of maximum distress: the kitchen table. Residential, PHP, and IOP programs frequently make use of therapeutic meal support. It is a way to help clients get through meals that may be difficult and help them process the emotions that come up. It also helps clients reorient to their hunger and fullness cues by inviting them to check in with their bodies both before and after meals. A hunger scale of 1 to 10, where 1 is "very hungry" and 10 represents "Thanksgiving full" can help clients get a sense of where they are and begin learning how to let that sense to guide their eating behavior.

Meal exposure. As previously discussed, the eating disorder makes certain foods and certain food groups feel wrong to eat. Other elements of meals can increase anxiety as well, such as having to make choices, not engaging in food rituals, and, of course, having a larger or smaller portion than you may be accustomed to. The point of meal exposure therapy is to expose clients to the food situations they fear so that their anxiety about it can naturally decrease—in other words, they get used to it. Exposure therapy is commonly used to treat phobias, like a fear of spiders: to get used to spiders, you wouldn't initially be asked to touch one, but you might look at pictures of spiders and, over time, you would acclimate with gradually more intense exposure. Similarly, meal exposure operates in a hierarchy: while you need to make sure that a person is getting adequate nutrition, you don't initially ask people who are used to eating nothing but carrots to sit down to a three-course meal. Instead, you ask them to expand their comfort zone just slightly, maybe by introducing another vegetable or a nutritional supplement like Boost. Meal exposure and therapeutic meal support often happen in tandem.

Meal plans. Meal plans help people receive adequate nutrition when they are in charge of some or all of their eating. To develop a meal plan, a dietitian collaborates with the client. Types of meal plans vary. A plan may lay out everything that someone is to eat or may operate on a system of exchanges. Exchanges offer the opportunity to make sure that nutritional needs are being met while allowing the client to have some choice. One example of an exchange system is making sure that meals have one carb, one piece of protein, and one veggie. Generally the earlier a client is in recovery, the more structured and less flexible the meal plan will be.

Intuitive eating. Intuitive eating is the eventual goal of most food recovery plans. Eating intuitively means that you are able to follow your body's cues for what and when to eat. You are able to eat when you are hungry and stop when you are full, considering all of the aspects of food that many of us take for granted: availability, taste, and nutritional value. Intuitive eating begins with the supportive guidance of a dietitian to make sure that important nutrient requirements are not being overlooked. As clients become more and more able to trust their body (and their body becomes more and more able to trust them to feed it well!), the amount of support can decrease.

Types of Providers

In your partner's journey to recovery, you might encounter several different types of treatment providers, including psychotherapists, dietitians, primary care doctors, and psychiatrists. Ideally these professionals will work together as a team, keeping each other informed of any significant changes and collaborating on care strategies. In the setting of a program such as inpatient, residential, IOP or PHP, teams keep informed by having regular meetings together as a part of their daily schedule. At the outpatient level of care, it is important that providers contact each other frequently if they are not in the same practice. They will need a release of information from your partner in order to do so, though.

PSYCHOTHERAPIST

A psychotherapist's job it is to help your partner understand and change the emotional and cognitive patterns that underlie the eating disorder. Psychotherapists can be psychologists, clinical social workers, or licensed professional counselors, based on the type of education and licensing that they have received. If your partner is unsure if a psychotherapist whom she is considering is licensed, she can contact the state licensing board. Some psychotherapists are covered by insurance, and some are not. If your partner's psychotherapist is not covered by insurance, you may still be able get some money back; ask your insurance company about out-of-network benefits for mental health.

DIETITIAN

A dietitian has been specifically trained in food science. It is important for your partner to be working with a registered dietitian, that is, a professional who has met the training and educational requirements for licensure. It is also important that your partner's dietitian have special expertise in the area of eating disorders. Much of the nutritional advice that would be appropriate for the general population would be highly inappropriate for someone who has had an eating disorder. Your partner may be weighed at the dietitian's office, or weighing may happen at the primary care doctor's office.

PRIMARY CARE DOCTOR

A primary care doctor, a medical doctor who is a generalist, should be a part of your partner's team. The doctor's job will be to monitor blood work for medical issues, such as electrolyte imbalance, dehydration, or heart problems. It can be difficult to find a primary care doctor who specializes in eating disorders. If you can, then great! If not, then make sure that your partner's primary doctor is willing to accept guidance from the rest of the team, embraces all-foods-fit and health-at-every-size philosophies, and will be careful about not letting your partner know her weight if that's a part of her recovery plan.

PSYCHIATRIST

If your partner requires medication to help him heal, he will have to get prescriptions from a psychiatrist, or a medical doctor who specializes in psychiatry. Sometimes psychiatrists offer psychotherapy too, and if your partner is considering this option, he should check whether his psychiatrist has had additional training in this area, as psychotherapy is often not well covered in medical school. Psychiatrists typically meet with patients for fairly short periods of time to check in on how things are going overall and to discuss any side effects from medication. As people become increasingly stable on a medication that works for them, they can check in with a psychiatrist less often.

Challenges in Recovery

Like all good things in life, recovery is not without its challenges. These can be both logistical and emotional, and acknowledging them ahead of time will help you in addressing them successfully.

Paying for Treatment

The truth is that treatment can be quite expensive, but there are options for help in paying for it all. The first step in determining how to pay for treatment is to contact your medical insurance company. Depending on the type of coverage, your insurance may pay for quite a bit of the expenses. Insurance companies often have lists of facilities and providers in their network, in which case the insurance will cover the cost of care, excluding copays and any deductible.

I urge you not to rule out psychotherapists or dietitians who do not accept insurance, however, especially if you are in a metropolitan area where few talented providers do. Insurance companies sometimes try to dictate the terms of treatment and place limits on how much treatment a therapist may provide, and so it may be the more ethical therapists who opt out of the system. You may also be able to find a lower cost option, such as going to a local training clinic with a sliding scale. Often universities that train psychotherapists have this type of center. Organizations such as the Manna Fund and Project Heal sometimes offer scholarships for treatment; visit their websites for more information (see resources).

Body Changes During Recovery

When the body gains back weight after a significant period, it first deposits fat in the midsection to protect our vital organs. This can take an especially difficult toll on those entering into recovery because belly fat is so strongly vilified in our culture. Your partner will need continued reassurance that body changes are a normal part of recovery and that the body will redistribute the weight, once it is able to trust your partner to feed it well and consistently. At the same time, in these conversations with your partner, you need to remember that commenting on your his actual body or body changes will not be helpful.

Stress on Relationships

Change is stressful. Even a positive change such as moving to a bigger house or starting a better job can be stressful. The same is true for eating disorder recovery. Your partner is trying new ways of relating to herself and her world, and this means that she is trying out things that she hasn't really done before. It can be easy to miss the mark at first. One patient told me, "When I was going into recovery, I was trying to figure out how to use my voice and not be so passive all the time. But I overshot the mark! Instead of being assertive and calmly holding my ground like I do now, I ranted and raved at my husband. But it was an important part of knowing how to move forward."

Here is another example of the strain that recovery can put on a relationship: Rosie and her husband started seeing me for couples therapy after Rosie had been in recovery for a year. They were arguing more as Rosie became increasingly depressed and emotionally distant. Her husband couldn't understand what was happening. Rosie was finally eating enough and had a whole team of people available to support her. Wouldn't she be over the moon? But actually Rosie's eating disorder had been keeping her from dealing with other issues such as career dissatisfaction and a difficult relationship with her sisters. Now that she was addressing those problems head-on, she had to deal with the feelings associated with them. She also had to mourn her eating disorder, which had done a lot to help her feel safe and comfortable for much of her life. Once Rosie's husband understood that she still had a great amount of emotional work to do, he was able to be a positive support and play an important role in her healing.

The Promise of Recovery

While it is important to acknowledge and plan for the difficulties associated with recovery, of course it also holds immense promise. As your partner disengages from the eating disorder and finds greater freedom and peace of mind, you will find a need to heal as well. It is my hope that you have learned new ways of thinking and being that you can carry forward beyond the pages of this book as you embark upon this journey. All change requires hard work and dedication, and there are likely to be frustrations along the way. Be patient with yourself, and remember that mistakes are opportunities to learn. My wish is that you and your partner find peace, freedom, and connection in your respective recoveries in the days to come.

Resources

EDReferral.com: This website allows you to search specifically for providers who have eating disorders experience within your area.

Ellyn Satter Institute. This organization aims to educate parents about healthy ways to approach food and eating with their children, based upon the writings of dietitian Ellyn Satter. http://www.Ellynsatter institute.org

FEAST (Families Empowered and Supporting Treatment of Eating Disorders): This organization provides education, training, and support for family members of loved ones with eating disorders. http://www .feast-ed.org

Lift the Shame: This live confidential support group is specifically geared toward pregnant women with eating disorders; it runs the third Sunday of each month from 7:00 to 8:00 p.m. EST. More information is available at http://www.timberlineknolls.com/information/support-groups/.

Manna Fund: This not-for-profit organization assists with financial aspects of treatment. http://www.mannafund.org

National Eating Disorders Association hotline: 1–800–931–2237

Project Heal: This not-for-profit organization offers scholarships for treatment as well as a peer-based mentor network for sufferers. http:// www.theprojectheal.org

Psychology Today: This directory helps you sort treatment providers by specialty, insurance, and location. Pictures and short blurbs are provided. More information is available at http://www.psychologytoday.com.

References

Ackard, D. M., S. Richter, M. J. Frisch, D. Mangham, and C. L. Crone-meyer. 2013. "Eating disorder treatment among women forty and older: Increases in prevalence over time and comparisons to young adult patients." *Journal of Psychosomatic Research* 74 (2): 175–78.

American Pregnancy Association. 2015. "Pregnancy and Eating Disorders." July. Retrieved from http://americanpregnancy.org/pregnancy-health/pregnancy-and-eating-disorders/.

American Psychiatric Association. 2013. *Diagnostic and Statistical Manual of Mental Disorders (DSM-V)*. 5th ed. Washington, DC: American Psychiatric Association.

Anorexia Nervosa and Related Eating Disorders. 2018. "Statistics: How Many People Have Eating Disorders?" Retrieved from https://www.anred.com/stats.html.

Brown, B. 2014. "Shame Vs. Guilt." *Brené Brown* (blog). January 13. https://brenebrown.com/blog/2013/01/14/shame-v-guilt/.

Bulik, C. M., E. R. Hoffman, A. Von Holle, L. Torgersen, C. Stoltenberg, and T. Reichborn-Kjennerud. 2010. "Unplanned Pregnancy in Anorexia Nervosa." *Obstetrics and Gynecology* 116 (5): 1136–40.

Centers for Disease Control and Prevention. 2018. "Weight Gain During Pregnancy." May 17. Retrieved from https://www.cdc.gov/reproductivehealth/maternalinfanthealth/pregnancy-weight-gain.htm.

Ellyn Satter Institute. 2018. "Raise a Healthy Child Who Is a Joy to Feed: Follow the Division of Responsibility in Feeding." Retrieved from https://www.ellynsatterinstitute.org/how-to-feed/the-division-of-responsibility-in-feeding/.

Gagne, D. A., A. Von Holle, K. A. Brownley, C. D. Runfola, S. Hofmeier, K. E. Branch, and C. M. Bulik. 2012. "Eating Disorder Symptoms and Weight and Shape Concerns in a Large Web-Based Convenience Sample of Women Ages 50 and Above: Results of the Gender and Body Image (GABI) Study." *International Journal of Eating Disorders* 45 (7), 832–44.

Goodman, E. 1999. "Ads Pollute Most Everything in Sight." *Albuquerque Journal*, June 27, C3.

Hong, Y. H., and S. Chung. 2018. "Small for Gestational Age and Obesity Related Comorbidities." *Annals of Pediatric Endocrinology and Metabolism* 23 (1): 4–8.

Hudson, J. I., E. Hiripi, H. G. Pope, and R. C. Kessler. 2007. "The Prevalence and Correlates of Eating Disorders in the National Comorbidity Survey Replication." *Biological Psychiatry* 61 (3): 348–58.

Hytten, F. 1985. "Blood Volume Change in Normal Pregnancy." *Clinics in Haematology* 14 (3): 601–12.

Institute of Medicine. 2007. *Preterm Birth: Causes, Consequences, and Prevention*. Washington, DC: National Academies Press.

Kabat-Zinn, Jon. 1994. *Wherever You Go, There You Are: Mindfulness Meditation in Everyday Life*. New York: Hyperion.

Keys, A., J. Brozek, A. Henschel, O. Mickelsen, and H. L. Taylor. 1950. *The Biology of Human Starvation*. 2 vols. Minneapolis: University of Minnesota Press.

Miller, A. M. 2016. "The Lasting Toll of an Eating Disorder: Fertility Issues." March 31. Retrieved from https://health.usnews.com/well ness/articles/2016–03–31/the-lasting-toll-of-an-eating-disorder -fertility-issues.

Morse, N. L. 2012. "Benefits of Docosahexaenoic Acid, Folic Acid, Vitamin D and Iodine on Foetal and Infant Brain Development and Function Following Maternal Supplementation During Pregnancy and Lactation." *Nutrients* 4 (7): 799–840.

National Eating Disorders Association. 2018a. "Eating Disorders in Men and Boys." Retrieved from https://www.nationaleatingdisorders .org/learn/general-information/research-on-males.

National Eating Disorders Association. 2018b. "Pregnancy and Eating Disorders: Complications of Disordered Eating During Pregnancy." Retrieved from https://www.nationaleatingdisorders.org/pregnancy -and-eating-disorders.

Norcross, J. C., P. M. Krebs, and J. O. Prochaska. 2011. "Stages of Change." *Journal of Clinical Psychology* 67 (2): 143–54.

Pinheiro, A. P., T. J. Raney, L. M. Thornton, M. M. Fichter, W. H. Berrettini, D. Goldman, K. A. Halmi et al. 2010. "Sexual Functioning in Women with Eating Disorders." *International Journal of Eating Disorders* 43 (2): 123–29.

Robert-McComb, J. J., L. Wilson-Barlow, and K. L. Goodheart. 2011. "An Overview of Eating Disorders." In *Eating Disorders in Women and Children: Prevention, Stress Management, and Treatment*, edited by K. L. Goodheart, J. R. Clopton, and J. J. Robert-McComb. 2nd ed. New York: CRC Press, Taylor and Francis Group.

Schaffer, J., and A. Robinson. 2015. "Binge Eating Disorder Statistics: Know the Facts." August 18. Retrieved from https://www.healthline .com/health/eating-disorders/binge-eating-disorder-statistics#1.

Sinha, S., and N. Warfa. 2013. "Treatment of Eating Disorders Among Ethnic Minorities in Western Settings: A Systemic Review." *Psychiatria Danubina* 25 (Suppl 2): S295–99.

Treasure, J., and G. Russell. 2011. "The Case for Early Intervention in Anorexia Nervosa: Theoretical Exploration of Maintaining Factors." *The British Journal of Psychiatry: The Journal of Mental Science* 199 (1): 5–7.

Vogel, G. 2015. "Weight Gain—and Loss—Can Alter Men's Sperm." December 3. Retrieved from http://www.sciencemag.org/news/2015 /12/weight-gain-and-loss-can-alter-men-s-sperm.

Ward, V. B. 2008. "Eating Disorders in Pregnancy." *British Medical Journal* 336 (7635): 93–96.

Dana Harron, PsyD, is a practicing psychologist in the Dupont Circle neighborhood of Washington, DC. She is founder and director of Monarch Wellness and Psychotherapy, a boutique practice that specializes in mind-body problems such as eating disorders, anxiety, trauma, fertility issues, and depression. Harron enjoys working with couples, and helping partners individually to understand eating disorders and learn how to give appropriate support. Harron completed her doctorate at Widener University's Institute for Graduate Clinical Psychology, where she was also the honored recipient of the Neubauer community service scholarship and the Empathy and Caring Award. She completed internships at the Renfrew Center and the Belmont Center, both in Philadelphia, PA.

Since then, she has engaged in a variety of professional activities ranging from co-leadership of a unit at the state hospital of Delaware to college counseling, and eventually to private practice. She is currently dividing her time between writing, speaking, clinical supervision, and, most importantly, to her direct client work. Harron has lectured at facilities such as Temple and George Washington University (where she is also serving as associate clinical faculty). She lives in Virginia with her husband and daughter, where she is an avid knitter and hiker.